THE
SILENT TRAVELLER
IN BOSTON

THE
SILENT TRAVELLER
IN BOSTON

Written and Illustrated by
CHIANG YEE

W · W · NORTON & COMPANY · INC ·

NEW YORK

T O

Walter and Jane Whitehill

Library of Congress Catalog Card No. 59-10935

PRINTED IN THE UNITED STATES OF AMERICA
FOR THE PUBLISHERS BY THE VAIL-BALLOU PRESS

1 2 3 4 5 6 7 8 9

Contents

Plates in Colour

Preface: Boston Dialogue

Place: Boston Common
Time: Just after lunch
Persons: One Irishman, one Italian, and one Chinese.

IRISH: So you have come from China to see Boston! What for? What do you want to see? Do you know Ireland then?

CHINESE: I have friends there and have gone there to see them on several occasions. I have been living in England since 1933. I stayed in Dublin twice.

IRISH: So you know Dublin. You must know St. Stephen's Green, Merrion Square, O'Connell Bridge, Guinness's and maybe you know Cork, Galway and Killarney too. Cork is the place where I was born. Cork is my birthplace.

ITALIAN: Oh, stop, enough of Cork, Cork, Cork this and Cork that. Nobody knows Cork but you. Who wants to know about Cork anyway?

IRISH: Half the people of Boston come from Ireland, and they all know Cork. Boston's Mayor came from Ireland. He can talk about Cork more than any of us. You can see how much he has done for Boston. Where did you come from, then? Where is your birthplace anyhow? I could not even pronounce it!

ITALIAN: What's so funny about it! My birthplace is called Pistoja, not far from where the great painter Leonardo da Vinci was born. I was born there seventy years ago and came to live in Boston more than forty years ago. Who cares whether you can pronounce my birthplace or not. You act like a funny man made of cork.

IRISH: Don't you dare to poke fun at my birthplace. I have lived in Boston as long as you, and I know you Italians.

ITALIAN: You said half the people of Boston are Irish. Do you know that the other half are Italian?

CHINESE: There is a Chinatown in Boston, isn't there?

IRISH: Yes, there is. But it's small. I like to eat there now and then. Chinese food is good.

ITALIAN: There are many good Italian restaurants in Boston. I like Italian food.

IRISH: There he is at it again.

ITALIAN: Who wants to eat Irish stew? Potatoes and potatoes. Mucky stuff.

IRISH: Better than spaghetti and tomato juice day in and day out, anyway.

CHINESE: I have heard that Boston is a City of Beans and Cod. And Boston clam chowder is famous. Isn't that so? And why?

IRISH: I cannot tell you. But Boston clam chowder is good.

CHINESE: Both you and your friend here have lived in Boston for more than forty years. Do you call yourselves Bostonians?

IRISH: Oh, no, far far from it. We don't want to be called Bostonians. We just live in Boston. Bostonians don't call us Bostonians anyway.

CHINESE: Who are Bostonians then?

IRISH: You don't see them in Boston. They don't live in Boston anymore.

CHINESE: Well, where can I see them? And what do they look like?

IRISH: They live outside Boston now. When they come to Boston, they stay indoors. They are queer ducks. What do you want to see them for?

CHINESE: What's queer about them? Don't they look like us?

ITALIAN: They talk queer. They walk queer. They don't laugh much. If they laugh, they laugh queer. Just like a Chinaman.

IRISH: Oh, oh, I beg your pardon for my friend.

CHINESE: Why apologize? Anybody can say what he thinks. I am glad that Bostonians are like Chinamen. I think I shall be able to see them. Or I don't need to see them. Just to see myself.

IRISH: Why do you want to see Bostonians? Are you a diplomat?

CHINESE: No.

IRISH: Are you a journalist, interested in politics?

CHINESE: No, I am not a journalist either. I don't think I could interest myself in any politics even if I wanted to.

IRISH: Why not? What do you mean? Everybody is and should be interested in politics.

CHINESE: I am different, for I have my difficulties. I mean, one has to live in a place long enough to know the politics of the place. For example, I lived in Dublin for a while. It took me time to find out who O'Connell was . . . well, I am *only* a traveller and just try to see what I can see when I come to a new place.

IRISH: Well, well, only a traveller. We are all travellers. You come from China, he from Italy, and I from Ireland. None of us has gone back home for a long time. We are all friends.

Friends outside our homelands. The world is a place for all travellers. Boston will like you to stay as we do. How long will you be in Boston?

CHINESE: A few months, I hope.

Arrival at Boston

Originally I lived in Mount Lu,
A dumbman well-acquainted with travels.
Riding the storm and braving the waves
    I reached the Western land,
Having seen all the winds and rains of the
    human world.

After twenty years' stay in Oxford, England,
I now drifted towards the Star-flag.
With no definite purpose
I stop at Boston temporarily,
Tracing at leisure the origin of the Yankees.

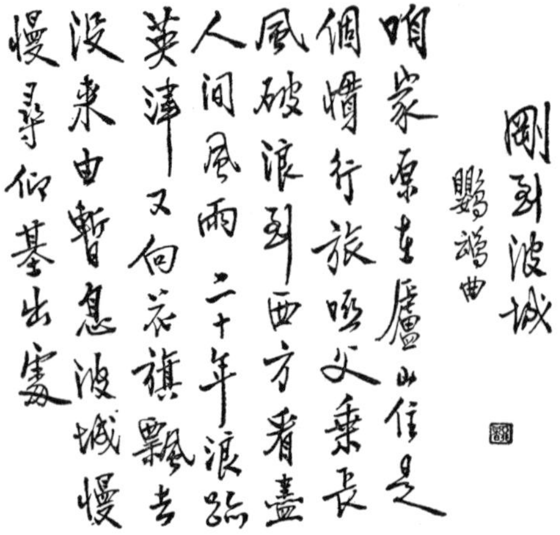

慢尋你基出家
沒來由暫息波城慢
英津又向茫旗飄去
人間風雨二十年浪跡
風破浪到西方看盡
個慣行旅�父乘長
咱家原本廬山住是

剛到波城
鸚鵡曲

THE
SILENT TRAVELLER
IN BOSTON

I

Boston Nose

M Y F A T H E R used to tell me when I was young at home that it is easy to train a man to be great if he has it in him to be great, but very difficult to teach a man to be a man among all men. He expected me just to be a man. Trying to be an ordinary man among men is still my goal. Being no historian I refrain from reading much of the history of the place where I happen to be; being no student of architecture I enjoy seeing interesting buildings from the layman's point of view. To be a man, an ordinary man, is not to be pretentious. In this spirit I am setting out to write about Boston.

In my travels I enjoy seeing similarities among all peoples rather than differences. I very seldom make a plan of campaign; I prefer to take what comes my way. Yet somehow in Boston I immediately had the whim to find out what a typical Bostonian looked like. I was encouraged in this whim by being urged on two different occasions to look at the Boston nose.

A week after my arrival in New York, I paid Dr. Walter Muir Whitehill my first visit in his office on the fourth floor of the Athenaeum. This was the beginning of our friendship. His magnificent mustache, unhurried gait, and serene manner all made an impression on me. He showed me the beautifully kept books on each floor, in which rarities from the early years of the library are mingled with the latest works on the subject. On the second floor I was introduced to Mr. David McKibbin of the art department, and then we had a look at the tea room, where from October to May one gets a cup of tea for three cents. With a smile, Walter said that although it was a relatively recent innovation, dating from 1913, people usually thought it had been in use for more

Back view of Boston Athenaeum

than a hundred years. "Bostonians like to keep old customs," he added. Outside the tea room we stood on the balcony for a while, looking down at the Granary Burying Ground with the silhouette of Park Street Church on the right.

Presently we returned to the fourth floor, and I was taken to see the George Washington Library in the trustees' room.

Pigeons in front of Park Street Church

Morning Haze over Beacon Hill

It contains Stuart portraits of the founders of the Athenaeum and a Houdon bust of Washington. There are many interesting items in the cases, one of which is a copy of the memoirs of Walton the highwayman, said to have been bound in his own skin. I could not help shuddering as I looked at it. Walter noticed and began to tell what a troublesome correspondence he had been involved in as a result of one visitor to the Athenaeum putting in print the remarkable statement that the library owned "the diary of George Washington, bound in his own skin."

I don't remember reading or seeing any book bound in human skin in either the Bodleian Library, Oxford, or the Bibliothèque Nationale, Paris. I looked at Walter and said that Chinese are safer, for Chinese books have always been bound in paper or silk, not yet in longer-lasting leather, though China is the country that first invented printing.

Passing through the fifth floor, we came to the busts of John Adams, John Quincy Adams, and Charles Francis Adams, directly ahead of us. I was immediately struck by their identical noses. I gave them a close look and resolved to study them further at my leisure.

On our way out to lunch at the Somerset Club in Beacon Street I remarked that the Athenaeum reminded me much of the London Library, though the Boston sunbeams do more to brighten up the well-ordered books and spotless chairs and desks than does the misty and foggy atmosphere which penetrates into the London Library. Walter agreed with me and told me that the Athenaeum is still a private institution, which was founded by a number of subscribers in 1807. I was then introduced to a few Athenaeum readers who were lunching there, too. I found the atmosphere inside the Somerset Club—the furniture, the carpet, the paintings on the walls, even the gait of the stewards—very similar to that of any club in London. When opportunity arose during the meal, I secretly cast my eyes round the dining room to study the noses of those present. I did the same at the annual dinner of the Colonial Society of Massachusetts at the Algonquin Club of Commonwealth Avenue, but that party was a bigger affair and I became confused at seeing so many noses.

After the New Year Professor and Mrs. W. G. Constable gave a dinner party at their house in Craigie Street, Cambridge, and I was asked to meet some of their friends. Professor Constable I had met long before the Second World War, when he was in charge of the Courtauld Institute in London. He arranged to take me round the painting section of the Boston Museum of Fine Arts, of which he was then curator. We first went round many of the European schools such as the Italian, Dutch, Spanish, and French, which, from the remarkable set of twelfth-century Catalan frescoes down to the nineteenth-century Impressionist painters, are well represented. Major works by Lorenzetti, Titian, Rubens, Poussin, Claude, Van Dyck, Rembrandt, El Greco, Velazquez, Corot, Delacroix, Degas, Monet, Manet, Renoir, Van Gogh, Gauguin, and other notable artists bring students to see them. I marvelled at the even, high quality of the whole collection. "This is where we can see the fine taste of the early Bostonians," remarked Professor Constable. "They really were remarkable," he continued. "In the late nineteenth century they began to collect the works of unknown artists like those Impressionists whom most people were attacking. Look at the value of their work now." Then as we walked along the corridor in the central dome of the building I was told to look at many small but good oil paintings by lesser European masters. They too bear evidence to the good taste of the early Boston collectors.

There is plenty, too, for the student of American art. We

came first to the Colonial and early Republican portraits. I think Gilbert Stuart must have created a record by painting the portraits of five American presidents. Copley's portrait of Samuel Adams (1722–1803), whose left arm seemed much shorter than the right one, caught my attention. Professor Constable said jokingly that Copley was not trained as a portrait painter. Copley painted Joseph Warren (1741–1775), who was killed on Bunker Hill, with his left arm somewhat out of proportion, too.

There are a number of good examples of the Hudson River School of landscape. Once when I was travelling with Van Wyck Brooks and William M. Ivins, a retired expert on prints from the Metropolitan Museum in New York, our talk unexpectedly centered on the Hudson River School of painting. We were driving on a bridge over the Housatonic River in Connecticut when Mr. Ivins remarked that most paintings of the Hudson River School were actually painted at different spots along the Housatonic River we were just crossing. He named some of the paintings. Van Wyck looked surprised. I had nothing to say, but now I looked all the more keenly at these paintings.

I was then taken to see the room of the forgotten period, 1815–1865, in American art. Professor Constable remarked that the exhibits here were quaint and unique, all done by people who had little or no art training but a burning enthusiasm to record what they saw and felt. They revealed that the artistic instinct and impulse are innate in man and can produce unusual and startling results. Maybe this forgotten period has caused the great popularity of Grandma Moses' work. Professor Constable, an Englishman, is to be congratulated on his interest in assembling and arranging this period in the American history of art so representatively.

Before introducing me to Mr. Peter Wick, who was to

show me Sargent's and Homer's water-colours, in which I am much interested, Professor Constable suggested that I should go and have another look at the American Colonial and early Republican portraits, saying: "Those faces there, except for the French Bishop Cheverus, could all be the faces of Bostonians living on Beacon Hill. Look at the noses in those portraits; they are Boston noses." The trailing sound of his gentle voice has never ceased ringing in my ears since I developed my earnest interest in the Boston nose.

In a well-known Chinese book of physiognomy, *Ma-yi-hsaing-fa*, the character of a man and his future are told from the features of his face. There are twenty-four types of human nose in the book and each has a special name such as "dragon nose," "tiger nose," "lion nose," "eagle nose," "onion nose," etc. A few words describe the character which goes with the respective noses. I thought three of the noses bore resemblances to those Boston noses I saw in the portraits in the Museum of Fine Arts, but soon I discarded the idea, for they were still the less-prominent Chinese noses.

One evening I attended a cocktail party given by Mr. and Mrs. Charles Mills of Washington, D.C., who were living in Louisburg Square at the time. "My father" declared one guest "was born here in 1841 and married here in 1866 and I was born here in 1869 and I am a Bostonian all right." Soon came another voice: "My father lived in Boston for seventy years but he was not considered a real Bostonian. I am fortunate that I was born in Boston. After I married I lived in Milton. After forty years there I began to be regarded as a Miltonian." Happy laughter greeted each of these statements. I did not ask on what condition one could be considered a Bostonian. I thought one of the outstanding qualifications must be the Boston nose. Before I could begin to make a study of the noses of the guests most of them had started moving away.

Mrs. Edward Cunningham has been very kind to me ever since our first meeting in the Somerset Club in October, 1952. Her grandfather, Robert Bennet Forbes, had been one of the leading shipmasters and merchants in the China Trade, and she has many Chinese friends. Before I came to see America, she said, she used to have copies of my books sent to the Library of Mills College, Oakland, California, in which she is much interested. After her eightieth birthday and when the New Year Festival was over, she had me to lunch in her hotel. I was the sole guest. I found myself saying that New York regards Boston as too conservative. My hostess refuted this. "For instance," she said, "the Somerset Club in Boston has a ladies' restaurant to which one can take young children for lunch or dinner, while the New York Cosmopolitan Club does not allow any child under fifteen to enter under any circumstances." After lunch my hostess asked where I was going. On hearing that I was going to the Museum of Fine Arts, she chuckled and told me to be sure to go and see the American room, for there I would see something which I could never see in any other museum in the world. I would find a group of people under a certain portrait and their family name would be that of the person in the portrait. All Bostonians were like that. They went to the museum to see their ancestors' portraits and never wanted to see any other pictures. We parted with a happy handshake. I felt pleased to have had this useful hint. Though a number of people were scattered in different rooms, I went straight to the rooms where the series of American Colonial and early Republican portraits hang. I met a group of four visitors on the way. Under the portrait of Captain James Greenleaf Otis a middle-aged lady was explaining something to three youngsters standing nearby.

When the other group of five came along they moved on without casting a look at the portrait the lady was talking about. Soon they stood under another portrait. I had to keep a little distance away lest I appear obtrusive. To my disappointment I was unable to compare the five noses with that

Looking at the family portraits

of the portrait. Nevertheless, I realised the unusual service which the Boston Museum of Fine Arts renders its visitors.

I paid a visit to the New England Historic Genealogical Society at Ashburton Place with a faint hope that I might get some indirect information about the Boston nose there. My arrival seemed to startle the person in the office, most probably because of my own nose. However he courteously asked what he could do for me. Whether he actually understood my hesitant answer or not, he began to relate the important purpose of the society and made me take a quick look round the library with its shelves of books and piles of pamphlets, which are all works on genealogy. There are about 200,000 books. The society, which is regarded as one of the most important of its kind in the United States, is ready to help without charge anyone from any part of the country in his or her genealogical puzzlement. People come every day for consultation. Jokingly I said that he could not have expected someone with a flat face like mine to walk in for a genealogical consultation. There were already a few people in the library when I arrived. One lady had a lot to tell about her family in a rather high-pitched voice. I did not prolong my intrusion. I felt bewildered. I said to myself that I came from a country whose ancestor worship is world-renowned, yet I had never seen so much reverence for ancestors anywhere in China as I saw in Boston.

Before attending a reception given by the Massachusetts Historical Society on the opening day of an exhibition of Adams Papers, I had dinner in New York with Francis Brown of the *New York Times*. We began to talk about my Boston trip. Mr. Brown said that he had once taken a taxi to the Massachusetts Historical Society but the driver had never heard of it. He then remarked that times are changing so fast that nothing will assume any importance in future. He told me that the society is the oldest historical society in the United States, founded in 1791, and that years ago everyone knew its building. When I arrived, the building was already full to capacity. Jane Whitehill and Mrs. John Adams took turns in serving tea at one end of the long table while another lady was busy at the other end. I exchanged a word or two with Walter Whitehill and David McCord, who were both in demand by other guests. I hardly knew anyone else. I felt quite busy, moving round. My presence there seemed to be as startling to many as it had been in the genealogical

Society. I cannot claim that I know anything about Massachusetts history. The Adams papers had for me a different interest from that which they presented to all the other guests in the building, who either knew the papers well or were related to the Adams family. I was amazed at the neat,

Indian Archer Weather Vane by Shem Drowne (1683–1774)

legible handwriting of the first John Adams copy of the Declaration of Independence from Jefferson's first draft. I was impressed by the enormous number of family documents, covering nearly two hundred years, which the Adams family had accumulated and preserved through nine generations. I was impressed at the perseverance of the first three Adamses, whose diaries covered in great detail every type of topic without a single day being missed. I come from a country where the family system has been the centre of everything under Confucius' principles of the Golden Mean and the Good Conduct of Life. But I doubt if such a collection of documents could be found in any family in China. It would seem as if we Chinese should make reservations in boasting of our family system, no matter how good it may have been in principle.

The first Adams had a great deal to do with the birth of

the great nation of the United States of America. Her independence was declared on July 4, 1776, which caused and is still causing other peoples of the world to refer to America as a young nation, compared with those in Europe and Asia. The words *young* and *old* really have no significance in this

The Massachusetts Historical Society (founded 1791)

connection but unfortunately the term *a young nation* in the popular mind implies a nation that is still rather unstable and can be sneered at. At least many of my compatriots used to use the term in that sense, without realising their own ignorance about the history of the country concerned. On the other hand, some self-conscious Americans whom I have met have used this phrase modestly when talking about the old civilisation of China. This has caused me embarrassment and I have felt impelled to remark that "America is not a young nation but her system of government started less than two hundred years ago." Before she declared her independence she had a colonial history of more than a hundred and fifty years. The early Pilgrims and Puritans were not natives of the land but a people with a historical background as long as any of the nations in Europe if not perhaps in Asia. They came with definite principles and ardent faith in life and mankind. Their minds were not feeble, young, unstable, or in other words as primitive as many founders of the nations in Europe and Asia, whose lives are mere legends. The Adams family came long before the birth of the first John Adams. His handwriting and wide knowledge did not come out of a blue moon. The first Adams and his colleagues were a group of great men who transplanted the civilisation of their ancestral country into a new land, working out a new system to suit the new environment, climate, and soil. The characteristics of American civilisation go back a long long way, just as many flowering plants in America had their origin in China. Many of them were hybrids. Hybrids, if good, remain good and flourish. All the Adams papers suggest to me a massive growth of well-cultivated flowers which had their horticultural origin in England and have become hybrids in America with unusual success. I am no student of history, but interested in reading history. Often I find that history books tend to be brief and to summarize events and that some historians show their particular bias for one thing or another. It is not always easy to visualise the growth of a nation, even a small one, within the limited area of one place, as one can do through reading the Adams papers in Boston. In Boston I feel that I can really read a history book which is not written in words but facts.

When I returned to the house of the friends with whom I was staying they joked that I had now become a Bostonian. My answer was that I could never be one even if I had all the other qualifications, for my nose remains somewhat flat. I had seen a large number of Boston noses that afternoon. The most striking one was that of Mr. John Adams, the President of the Massachusetts Historical Society. I thought his face familiar, and it took me no time to realise that he had the same shape of nose as his great-great-grandfather, President John Adams of the United States. I now am satisfied as to the Boston nose; it is the type of nose possessed by Mr. John Adams, President of the Massachusetts Historical Society. I do not want to have him troubled by the curiousity of my readers. But I myself am looking forward to the pleasure of seeing the youngest generation of the Adamses.

II

Boston Hill

F o r m e , Boston Hill is Beacon Hill. There are other hills
in Boston such as Bunker Hill and Copp's Hill. I only know
Beacon Hill and perhaps know it better than other parts of
Boston after living on it for a short while. One's life is very
short in the eternity of time. Why should one bother oneself
with the little things about the place where one is living,
while so many big and important matters like the threat of
another world war with A-bomb and H-bomb and thousands
of people being killed without reason are discussed in the
papers and on the radio? Very few can give a clear answer
to this question. Not I at any rate. It is the way of us mortals.
Beacon Hill lived before it earned its name and it will still
live even if it undergoes a change through some inconceiva-
ble happening. It is one of the most *livable* places that I have
met in my travels.

It was my friends Gladys and Van Wyck Brooks who suggested that I should try to find a place to live on Beacon Hill.
After I had spent a few days with the Yang family in Cambridge, Lien-Sheng (head of the family and Professor of
Chinese at Harvard) took me to Boston. No. 69 Pinckney
Street was the third house at which we knocked, and in no
time I was installed there. I cannot relate the history of the
house, but its sedate air and surroundings were unusually
agreeable to me. As a self-appointed traveller these many
years, I have never found living quarters a problem, except
that they have had to match my means. Luxurious hotels

would not entertain me, for I could not entertain their staff. Some fine residential areas have no experience of having a travelling stranger in the house for a while and I have never known how to present myself to them. A few places where I have stayed have been some distance away from the center of the city or town, but from Beacon Hill stretch streets to all parts of Boston. Above all, it is a hill, neither too high nor too low, providing me with the delicious novelty of walking up and down slowly instead of moving to and fro along monotonous flat streets with nothing to see in front or behind. After a few days I discovered that each street on Beacon Hill has its own character, although all the houses are built of red-brick.

In the entrance hall of the Widener Memorial Library of Harvard University are four modelled maps of Cambridge from the days when Harvard University was founded in 1636 to the present day. The first one of these maps clearly shows that Beacon Hill used to be a three-pronged eminence of earth across the Charles River, the most conspicuous object in the landscape that the first settlers saw when they made their final short migration in September, 1630. The three hills were then called *Trimountaine,* from which comes the name of the street, *Tremont.* The *new* State House with its gilded dome was built on the lower part of the hill in 1795 to distinguish it from the old State House on Washington Street. Owing to the rapid growth of manufactures in the beginning of the nineteenth century Boston developed further and further. A great change took place on Trimountaine. In 1799 one prominent part of the west side called Mount Vernon was levelled down and the earth was used to fill in the river and to raise Charles Street to its present level. Later the central peak, Beacon Hill, was lowered to fill the millpond at the foot, and finally, in 1835, the other prominent part on the east side, called Cotton Hill, was flattened to make Pemberton Square, on which the Court House now stands. From this I can see that the water of Charles River flowed close to the lower end of Pinckney Street on one side of Beacon Hill and that Washington Street was at the foot of the hill on the other side. Beacon Hill used to be the head of the peninsula and was all the area of Boston there used to be. The making of American history began in Boston and Beacon Hill played its part.

It was my friend Dr. David T. W. McCord, Executive Secretary of the Harvard Fund Council, who took me to the Widener Memorial Library and gave me the chance of studying those maps. I learnt that it took one hundred and ninety pick-and-shovel men with sixty yoke of oxen several months to level Cotton Hill. Each man was paid about a dollar a day but the experienced ox-drivers had board in addition to their pay. That was a little more than a hundred years ago. It would certainly take less people and fewer days to accomplish the task in our present machine-age. But I am inclined to think that the same spirit which made the early settlers set about removing hills has continued to make Americans look on nothing as impossible. The tall skyscrapers on the levelled, solid surface of the huge Manhattan rock had their origin here on Beacon Hill.

There was a sacred Cod in the State House that I must go and see, according to one friend of whom I had made an enquiry about Boston cod and beans. Having arrived at the State House and been immediately bewildered to see so many battle flags in the entrance hall, I was directed upstairs. There I passed a few people who were bending to read the Bradford manuscript—the story of the Plymouth Pilgrims, written by Governor Bradford himself—in a glass case. A uniformed guard, the third of whom I enquired my way, said: "What, the wooden Codfish? Over there in the Hall of the Representatives." From his manner of speaking, I guessed that not many people came to see the Cod. I hesitated to enter the hall for a few gentlemen in formal dress, looking like possible Representatives, were deep in discussion. A meeting seemed just to have ended. One of them kindly beckoned me in and then pointed to the codfish, while still continuing his conversation. I found a big piece of wood, cut in the shape of a codfish, painted black, with white or red curved lines for the scales and a white dot for the eye. It was hanging above the raised platform of the hall. There were no words of explanation underneath it. The group of Representatives had left the hall, but the one who had beckoned re-entered. He explained to me that that wooden codfish originated from an order, in 1784, that a codfish be suspended "in the room where the House sat as a reminder of the importance of Cod Fishing for the welfare of this Commonwealth." It was first suspended in the room in the old State House, down in Washington Street, in pursuance of the resolution of 1784. But more than a century later, in 1895, an order to remove the ancient symbol of a codfish from the old hall to the new was carried out by a committee of fifteen who proceeded to the Old State House, wrapped the symbolic wooden cod in the American flag, laid it on the shoulders of two of the bearers, and walked proudly in state through Washington Street and then up here to Beacon Hill. It must have been a grand procession. I supposed that was why this wooden symbol was called the *sacred* codfish. As it was *sacred* I thought there must be some special ritual or ceremony performed before the start of each meeting or on some fixed date. The answer was "No." Apparently not many Representatives give it a look on entering the hall: "I have not seen anything like this codfish in any other state house in the U.S.," I remarked. "Boston is unique," came the answer. I thanked my kind informant. And I enquired if I might climb the dome to see the view, for I had read somewhere that years ago Enoch Wines of London, England, made the following remark after he had seen the view from the dome of Boston's State House: "I have visited many elevated points in the four continents of Europe, Asia, Africa, and America; and I declare that none of the prospects thus obtained are superior, and fewer still equal, to that enjoyed from the State House at Boston." It was not possible for me to climb it that morning, but something could be arranged, so I was told. I thought I had better leave that view of Enoch Wines' to my imagination. I do not know when Enoch Wines climbed the dome. He must have been in America before the Rockefeller Center or the Empire State Building went up. I would like to imagine he saw the view before the demolition of Cotton Hill or even of Mount Vernon. At any rate, the view he had must have been very different from what I saw from the top of John Hancock Building. Boston, like most cities, is spreading.

I did not climb the dome of the State House that Charles Bulfinch designed, for I had been taken up to see another important Bulfinch building in Boston—the Massachusetts General Hospital. Apart from the importance of Boston State House as a governmental building, it seemed to me the greatest monument that could perpetuate an architect's name. I heard much of the Bulfinch front and the Bulfinch interior. He not only designed an original and successful model for the State Houses of almost every State of America but was chosen, as I learned, to complete the design and the building of the Capitol that now stands for all to admire at Washington D.C. It was Dr. John Constable, son of Professor W. G. Constable of the Boston Museum of Fine Arts, who suggested that he would like to show me the hospital building. He considers the view from the roof there the best in Boston. I arrived in good time for the appointment. Doctors always have *time* on their minds. John did not spend long showing me the room, not far from the roof, where the first dental operation with the use of anaesthetics took place. A minute later we were on the roof. I agreed with John that, seen from the roof of the Massachusetts General Hospital, Boston State House sits solidly and firmly at the waist of Beacon Hill and becomes "the hub of the solar system," as Oliver Wendell Holmes once remarked, while the water of the Charles stretches out and out to the infinite sea. The old and the new blended unforgettably. It was not a mere bird's-eye view like a photograph of any big city taken from an aeroplane. I have seen many an air-photograph of cities and none of them really show any character. But the character of Boston could be seen from the roof of the Massachusetts General Hospital.

On our way down I tried to read an inscription on the wall of the room where the first use of anaesthetics was made. John left me to finish reading by myself, for he had to attend to his patients. I thanked him and presently returned to Pinckney Street with much to think about. The following from Dr. M. A. DeWolfe Howe's pen interests me:

The monument to William Thomas Green Morton in the Boston Public Garden may be taken to represent the award of posterity in the dispute between the two chief claimants to the glory of the discovery. . . . After coming to Boston Dr. Morton studied under Dr. Jackson. Later, when seriously considering the possibilities of anaesthesia in dentistry, he went to Jackson for advice, and the use of rectified sulphuric ether was recommended. This was not a discovery of Jackson's. Several years before, acting on a suggestion of Sir Humphry Davy, he had himself inhaled sulphuric ether, with the result of unconsciousness.

He had not tried it for the prevention of pain. Morton immediately proceeded with the experiment, first upon himself, then, September 30, 1846, on a patient willing to attempt unconsciousness during the extraction of a tooth. On the next day Morton hastened to Jackson with the news of his success. This time Jackson advised the dentist to lay the matter before the surgeons of the Massachusetts General Hospital. He did so, and on October 16, 1846, was permitted to administer ether to a patient upon whom Dr. John C. Warren performed an operation with such success that the painless removal of a tumor and the amputation of a leg, within three weeks of Dr. Warren's initial venture, established beyond doubt the inestimable value of the new achievement.

While I was in charge of the Chinese Section in the Wellcome Historical Medical Museum at Euston, London, from 1938–40, I was often told that the anaesthesia was first discovered in Boston. So neither Berlin, nor London, nor Paris —but Boston—was a pioneer in lessening the suffering of man.

The importance of Beacon Street on Beacon Hill is unquestionable. It is a beautiful street, open on one side to Boston Common and the Public Garden just as one side of Princes Street in Edinburgh is open to the Gardens and the Castle Rock. Unlike Edinburgh's Princes Street, the buildings in Beacon Street are not commercial premises but fine houses. Holmes called it "the sunny street that holds the sifted few." "The sifted few" are not all Holmeses nor Cabots. The house of William Hickling Prescott was pointed out to me at 55 Beacon Street, where Thackeray had his first dinner in America and where he presented a copy of his *Esmond* to the noted historian.

What interested me most was the very English-looking doors with brass lion-heads as door knockers in the wall outside the Somerset Club. I thought at first that these doors were the main entrance, but as I never went in by them when I came to join some luncheon or dinner party, I soon discovered that they had in earlier years led to the kitchen, but now led nowhere. Walter Whitehill told me that some years ago when flames suddenly burst out of a pan of deep

Somerset Club

fat in the kitchen of the Somerset Club, the firemen were told by the doorman to enter by this service door. This aroused the indignation of certain newspapermen, who condemned the "exclusiveness" of the Club. Actually the firemen could not have reached the fire quickly enough by the members' entrance. I laughed when I found that the service entrance has the most English-looking door of all. I have not yet experienced "exclusiveness" among the Beacon Hillers, and in fact found them often relating anecdotes and tales at their own expense, although I do not think they have gone so far as to establish a joke factory, as it is said the Aberdonians have done, to produce jokes about themselves in order to attract people to come and see the clean city of Aberdeen.

Beacon Street is a sunny street and the houses that face the Common and the Public Garden get the most sun. I have seen their windows shining in the sun with mysterious and alluring colours, chiefly purplish. At first I thought they were reflecting the sunset or the collective mellowness of the red-brick walls. Presently I discovered that the glass itself was purplish. Someone erroneously told me that Mayflower descendants had the privilege of using purple windows in their houses. Someone else claimed that the occupants of those houses with purple windows were not all Mayflower descendants and that a certain house had had some purple glass put in the windows not very long ago. At last I established that a certain amount of glass was ordered from England for the new houses being built on Beacon Hill from 1816–1824. After the houses had been up for years, the glass, being exposed to the hot sun in Boston, underwent a slow natural chemical transformation from being without colour to being purplish. This unexpected change did not annoy the occupants of the houses, who were pleased to see their curtains, ceilings, and rooms enhanced with mellow light and purplish splendour. Thus a fashion arose for purple glass. But I am not so sure that the fashion was new, for I have read that Yuan Mei (1716–1798), an eighteenth-century Chinese poet, liked to have purple glass in his famous garden, Sui-yuan, in Nanking. Glass was not made in China in those days. It came to China from abroad, most likely from England. In other words, England had already produced purple glass before 1816.

There were more purple-glass windows along Chestnut Street and other streets on Beacon Hill, but they were not easy to detect from the outside like those along Beacon Street. The names "Chestnut," "Spruce," "Willow," "Ce-

Acorn Street

dar," "Walnut," and "Acorn" Streets interested me; were such trees actually cut down to make room for houses and streets? Many trees still grow on the hill, though in an orderly way and not profusely as they may have done before. Beautiful tall elms line both sides of Mount Vernon Street and give it distinction. It is wide and has pavements for leisurely walking. Cars come and go more frequently than on the other streets, for it is directly connected with the back thoroughfare of the State House. If Beacon Street resembles Edinburgh's Princes Street, Mount Vernon is, then, like its George Street. Most houses along George Street are in Georgian style, built in grey granite, and wear the cold and bracing air of Edinburgh. The red-brick houses along Mount Vernon Street breathe the serene, mellow atmosphere of Boston. Acorn Street is the narrowest, therefore the quietest of all the streets.

Each house in Mount Vernon Street seemed to have a story to tell me. I found that the doors of two houses, Nos. 78 and 108, do not face directly to the street like the rest, but are slightly slanted towards the southwest. This reminded me of houses in my native city with a similar irregular arrangement of their entrance doors. They were so arranged under the Chinese ancient belief in "Feng-shui" or "wind-water"—that which cannot be seen and cannot be grasped. By the old geomantic system of the Chinese, it is possible to determine the desirability of sites for tombs, houses, or cities, from the configuration of such natural objects as rivers, trees, and hills, and to foretell with certainty the fortune of any family, community, or individual, according to the spot selected; it is possible for the geomancer to counteract evil influence by good ones, to transform straight and noxious outlines into undulating and propitious curves, and generally to rectify the influences of nature, which if left to themselves would entail ruin upon all concerned. As a rule, before the construction of a house, whether big or small, a noted geomancer would be called to have a good look at the piece of land on which the house was to be built, and to decide in which direction the main entrance should face. If there was no choice, the geomancer would try to counteract the evil influence by shifting the doors to a slightly slanting position. Any house-owner hopes for good fortune, so every

Chinese who could afford to build a house for himself and family consulted the geomancer, who was a special type of professional man in China up to thirty or forty years ago. I don't think geomancers will be found in the China of today. When Europeans and Americans began to build foreign

West Cedar Lane

houses in China with doors on any side, the Chinese geomancers shouted that evil influences which they were powerless to counteract would upset the old tradition of all Chinese houses, and there was no more demand for their knowledge. Quite a number of the older generation in China have tended to agree with the geomancers' opinion in the light of their experiences in the past fifty years. I still wondered why Nos. 78 and 108, Mount Vernon Street, had entrances different from the rest.

I was privileged to enter two of the twenty-two houses in Louisburg Square. One was No. 12, where Mr. and Mrs. Charles Mills asked me to join their cocktail party before they moved to San Francisco, the other No. 16, where I paid Dr. Mark A. DeWolfe Howe several visits. Mr. Van Wyck Brooks had asked me to see him as soon as possible, for he, being author of more than thirty books on New England, would be able to tell me much about Boston. Dr. Howe had already passed his eighty-ninth birthday when I called in October, 1952. He told me that as his sight had failed, he now read books on gramophone records provided by the Library of Congress at Washington, D.C., a most remarkable institution. He then told me that he had recently written an article about the late Miss Alice Bache Gould, a remarkable lady who had spent years in identifying "The names of every sailor who was with Columbus." This started my inquiries about the statue of Columbus in the Square garden. He knew all about it. While Louisburg Square was being built a rich Greek merchant sent to Athens for a statue of Aristides the Just. Upon its arrival he asked his neighbours if they would agree to let him put Aristides in the center of the Square among the trees. A meeting was held and a Committee of three was appointed to decide the matter. The decision was that Aristides, the Greek, should be put at one end and another statue, Columbus, the father of all the Americans, should be set at the other end. The merchant agreed and so the two statues are in the Square now. They have been there for nearly a hundred years. It was now clear to me that not every early occupant of Louisburg Square had been a Mayflower descendant.

I do not know how we came to talk of Prescott's noctograph which I had seen in a show case at the Massachusetts

Historical Society. Dr. Howe has told the story of it in one of his early books. The noctograph was Prescott's own invention, after he had been blinded as a result of having a piece of bread thrown in his eye by a fellow student during a student brawl. I remarked that from what I had read about Oxford, in the medieval days Oxford students sometimes used to engage in fights too. Before I bowed to take leave, Dr. Howe kindly suggested taking me to lunch at the Tavern Club to meet some friends of his there. Then he told me that during the First World War, Bishop Lawrence entertained the Archbishop of York in that club. At that time there was a small restaurant in the front of the club called the "Black Cat." The two bishops seated themselves in the Black Cat instead of in the Club. After a good while they were extracted. I remember going with the late Professor John Wheatley to the Athenaeum Club, London, which is full of bishops, and hearing that bishops very seldom knew where they were and always thought they were in their Bishop's palaces.

One side of Louisburg Square is on Pinckney Street, and whenever I went down the hill to the riverside or to the Common I lingered a moment or two in the Square. The tranquil air there never tried to hurry me on. Cars must have come through the Square often and I saw cars parked by the railings of the Square garden, but I never saw a car in motion. It seemed as if the occupants of the houses were so perfectly contented that they never wanted to go anywhere. This brought me a refreshing stillness of mind from the midst of the life of a modern city. I made a number of rough sketches of various doorways and angles of the Square. I tried to sketch the Square as a whole from Mount Vernon Street. From there the Square revealed itself to me to be higher on the east side than on the west, so that the houses along Pinckney Street are in full view on winter mornings. In this natural arrangement the Square could be more easily seen as a whole than many Squares in London, which seldom show their faces in full. The houses reminded me of those near the Albert Hall in the South Kensington area. Nevertheless, I feel that Louisburg Square has a distinction of its own with its full face, its optimistic serenity, its independent system of upkeep by which the twenty-two house proprietors meet annually and tax themselves for the purpose. I have heard of nothing like that in London.

The little garden in the center of the Square endeared itself to me. One warm night I lay awake in bed until at last I got up and went out for a stroll as I used to do in my homeland on summer nights years ago. England had offered me not one chance of doing this in my eight thousand nights there. In China when summer nights were warm we stayed in the garden at the back of our house, sat on the rocks, or lay down under the trees or walked round the little pond in the center until the coming of a cool spell in the early hours. The house in Pinckney Street where I lodged had no garden, so I slipped into Louisburg Square. The moon high above was more inclined to cast her glance on the Common than on where I was standing. She made the roof-line of the houses stand out clear and unmistakable for me. She did the same to every leaf on the trees. Not a leaf vibrated. The silence could be felt. Unlike the winter-night shadows which suggest hungry prowling creatures, the spring nights full of buoyancy, and the autumn nights with their subtle spell of life, this long summer night brought an enchantment which I had only experienced in my younger days. Some blades of grass stood out singly in the moonlight but many were darkened into a black mass between the tree-trunks. Gazing at that black mass here and there in the little garden of the

Square I detected tiny lights winking and sparkling. They were fireflies. At the same time my ears were filled with a soft music as intoxicating as that of familiar tunes I had heard in faraway Kiukiang. It was the chirp of crickets. The very presence of the fireflies and crickets created a sentiment in me too poignant to tell, a sentiment my English friends could not appreciate, for few of them know fireflies and crickets, a sentiment my American friends might brush aside as unimportant as they have known fireflies and crickets since they were young, whereas for me they stir memories of twenty-four years ago. This sentiment will be strange to many Chinese too; particularly those born within the past thirty years will not be able to understand, for life in China has undergone much change, natural and unnatural, since the First World War. I accept *change* in life as a matter of course and seldom expect to see change being swept away and old things being restored. Yet a summer night in Louisburg Square had brought back to me my childhood in my old home garden, laughing, chasing, quarrelling with girl and boy cousins while we tried to catch fireflies or to play the cricket-fight game. A sweet sentiment! After returning I composed the following little poem:

> Around the Square red-brick buildings
>   hide behind tall trees;
> The intensity of summer heat is decreasing
>   gradually.
> Dots of fireflies compete to appear in
>   front of me
> As if we had known each other, recalling my
>   younger days.
> How lucky that we meet again under this sky
>   beyond China seas!

Hundreds and thousands of thoughts
Flash like lightning.
Happy and sorrowful moments, no use to trace
    back.
When did we see perfection in human affairs?
The quietness of the night with the purity
        of the breeze desire to break my contemplation;
Moving away aimlessly, I return for a sound sleep.

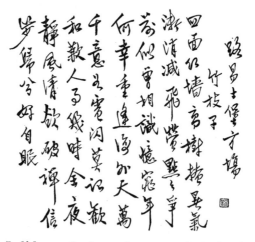

Though I did not find much external similarity between Louisburg Square and Russell Square, I think the interiors of the houses must be very similar, for I have been told many times that No. 20 Louisburg Square was chosen for the filming of Thackeray's *Vanity Fair*. Thackeray's reaction to his first taste of American oysters and his Boston lectures are still talked about today. Dickens' stay with his friend in Charles Street is still spoken of too, even if many Americans resent the manner in which he wrote about America. Surely many noted English writers must have visited Boston since the days of Dickens and Thackeray. Why are there no anecdotes about their visits? A "change" has taken place in Boston, I venture to state. This change, like that taking place in other parts of the earth, seems to me inevitable owing to the ever-increasing human population. In a small city, people's behaviour is noticed. When the population becomes dense, a few names might appear one hour and be lost again the next hour. It is fortunate for Boston that she had so many illustrious names in her less populated days!

View from Pinckney Street

During my whole stay in Pinckney Street I enjoyed the feeling of living not too high up a hill. Walking down in the early morning I would imagine that the very thin mist was lifting me up in the air while it dispersed, and I would reach the lower ground without any effort. More than once I felt that the massive buildings of the Massachusetts Institute of Technology were playing some trick with me when I came down to the Embankment Road from Pinckney Street. They looked like a small white plastic model of a Greek

Temple lying on the opposite shore of the Charles River, and I felt I could easily handle them. Some evenings they turned reddish or purple under the gorgeous sunset sky. One morning they were there, clear and bright; the next morning there would be no trace of them. Had I not been taken round the Institute by Dr. Chao Kuo-chun and had I not known its great reputation for research, I could easily have taken its appearance for a mirage.

In the daytime, car traffic was audible occasionally, but footsteps were to be heard all the time. They emphasized the quietude on the hill rather than disturbing it. I met people on my walks rarely and encountered almost none coming home late at night. There was no occasion for me to rush up the hill; there was always someone accompanying me home on moonlit nights. I had a companion who moved as I moved. It was the Boston moon. Such was my joy in my stay on Beacon Hill.

III

Boston Christmas

O f a l l the old festivals, that of Christmas awakens the strongest and most heartfelt of associations." So says Washington Irving in his "Travelling at Christmas." Having been brought up in a strict Confucian family I knew very little about Christmas until my first experience of it in England in 1933. I had only then been in London for five months. A newly-made friend invited me to spend Christmas with his family not far outside London. Before setting out for my friend's house I wanted to read something about Christmas. I remembered having had to struggle with Dickens' *A Christmas Carol* when learning English as a boy at school in China. Our teacher was not a Christian and could not explain much to us and there were too many hard words to learn. I did not want to turn to that again. Curiously enough I found little else written on the subject by English authors, but instead I came upon Washington Irving's "Travelling at Christmas," "Christmas in an old Hall," and "Christmas merriment," and having read these, I set off full of expectation. My most vivid memory now is of my hostess, a buxom lady of sixty, as she stood at one end of the dining table with sleeves rolled up and carving-knife and fork in hand, preparing to carve the mountain of turkey and outsize Cumberland ham which were placed in front of her. She beamed happily while carving, and I smiled with the other seven of us, though my mind went back to my birthplace in China, where no knife was allowed to be seen outside the kitchen of my old Confucian family and according to Confucius, a "Gentleman keeps away from the kitchen." There was not much left of either turkey or ham after each of us had had a second helping. I often thought of that meal during the food-rationing years of the Second World War.

After the dinner we all sat round a huge fireplace in the central hall, a little distance away from a large Christmas tree, which was elaborately decorated and had a number of beautifully-wrapped parcels on it. Two younger members of the family had to go to bed before we unpacked our Christmas presents. They had to wait until their presents had been brought down the chimney during the night, according to the custom. My hostess began to tell me something about the Christmas story and Christmas customs while my host laughingly clinked glasses with the other guests. Presently each of us had to provide an item of entertainment. When it came to my turn, I managed to relate a Chinese story about our Chinese New Year Festival. Very suddenly my hostess stood up and asked all of us to join hands and sing. I had to be silent but I moved my arms as briskly as the rest. A big bunch of mistletoe hung under the lamp in the center of the room. Our movements brought us closer and closer to it, and soon kissing and laughter were mingled. Many escaped. I learnt that according to the custom any lady who stood under the mistletoe must be kissed. When I think of it now, I realise that I got that information much too late.

As far as Boston Christmas is concerned, Thomas Wentworth Higginson wrote in 1911: "In those days, [1845] Christmas gifts were not the customary thing; but the making of presents was reserved until New Year, although I find an account of celebrating Christmas by taking part in charades and dancing on that evening—ending by joining Levi

Louisburg Square

The First Christian Science Church in snow

Thaxter (afterwards Celia Thaxter's husband) and giving a serenade to a certain Cambridge belle." This at least proves that Christmas was not commonly celebrated in Boston a century ago.

The most important festival of the year in New England is Thanksgiving Day. I was fortunate to have Mr. and Mrs. John Nichols to take me to Mrs. Cobb's house for my first Thanksgiving dinner at Willow Street, Beacon Hill. It was a purely family gathering, for the Nicholses are related to the Cobbs. I felt a little out of the scene, but I did have my first taste of pumpkin pie. Pumpkin pie may be an everyday dish to many, but to me it was new. I doubt if many English people know of it. I did not see a pumpkin in all my years in England. The word "pie" has always interested me since I came to live in the West. There is no pie in Chinese cooking. But there are many kinds of pies in England. M. Boulestin, owner of the famous Boulestin Restaurant in Covent Garden, London, and an authority on the French cuisine, says; "An English cook throws away more food in a week than a French one would in months." I cannot agree with him, for I don't think an English cook throws away much, otherwise there could not be so many pies. Now pumpkin pie is an addition to my list of pies. I believe that pumpkin pie is an essential item in the American Thanksgiving dinner, as the pumpkin was one of the first vegetables that grew and was harvested by the Pilgrims.

In my first month, November, in Boston, I was disillusioned to find the Christmastide already sweeping along Boston Common and Washington Street. Nowadays Christmas is certainly brought to one's notice before one can make use of one's intelligence. Apart from the multicolored decorations in the department stores and the many well-dressed women carrying piles of boxes to and fro, I heard a new sound along Washington Street. It came from the bells rung by a number of Salvation Army Santa Clauses. I thought this sound peculiar to Boston, for I had not heard it on the other side of the Atlantic Ocean. I now know that the same type of bellringers are active in New York, but the sound cannot be heard as clearly there as in Boston. In England I had always tried to explain to my young English friends that they must be patient, as there was only one Santa Claus who had to have time to make his round of all the chimneys. Young children in Boston would regard me as the eternal inscrutable Chinese if I said the same to them, for they could tell me how many Santa Clauses they had encountered inside and outside the department stores along Washington Street.

A white deer symbolises longevity in Chinese conventional Taoist thought. In our forefathers' belief its fur turns white when it reaches 1500 years of age. It is considered a very rare animal, only to be found in the Taoist Paradise in Heaven. Though I have seen an ancient Chinese painting of a white deer on silk, I never saw a live one in China. Yet there were eight of them in a wired enclosure on Boston Common, making a unique item of decoration for the Christmas story at Christmas time. The mayor of Boston or one of his subordinates must have had divine power to get hold of those white deer—at least a power as divine as some Chinese Taoist immortals. I went to Boston Common just to gaze at them and to sketch them many a time. But I never once heard a child ask if the white deer would draw the sledge for Santa Claus.

Many big figurines and models of Nativity scenes were arranged on Boston Common. There were always some people, both young and old, strolling around them. One afternoon I watched two young children feeding the pigeons: one let all the birds fly round his head, arms, and feet, while the other preferred to feed only one pigeon at a time and kept shoving the other birds away. Their different attitudes were most interesting to watch and their behaviour would have delighted any artist. I regretted that I had no paper with me on which to make sketches. Suddenly a white-haired lady

walked towards me and told me with a firm voice not to encourage the children to feed the pigeons. Before I could reply to this astonishing reprimand, she went on to say that there used to be very few pigeons in Boston but that they had bred and bred until they were all over Boston; they interfered with the traffic, they disfigured the Common, and they soiled the benches and paths; one day they would drive everybody away from Boston. After a pause, she added that she meant they would drive all Bostonians away. I was still speechless. Unexpectedly she asked whether I was a Christian and if so to which denomination I belonged. I had not time to answer before she warned me not to believe a word said by the people who had arranged the Nativity scenes on Boston Common. This startled me more than ever. Shortly she said good-bye to me and left. It was an awkward encounter.

Long before Christmas Eve, red candles burned each evening in almost every window of the houses upon Beacon

Hill. I used to walk up the hill by way of Charles Street and Mount Vernon through Louisburg Square to Pinckney Street, or through Chestnut Street to Pinckney Street. Though the street lights were quite strong, the candle-light on both sides seemed to illuminate the street with an ethereal tint of red which made the street lights unimportant. As the houses were built along the slope of the hill, the window lights did not confuse each other, but each had its own significance. I did not meet many people walking up the hill at night. I felt myself strolling along with a tranquil, mellow air as if I were floating slowly and aimlessly in the form of a butterfly, hovering in the evening glow of sunset, seeking a restful quarter for the night. The red-brick walls of the houses contributed to the scene, which seemed far removed from the noises down the hill beyond the Common. Beacon Hill with all the window candle-lights at Christmas time is unique.

Perhaps I should not spoil matters by telling that the candles were not real. But every American knows that a natural development of using electricity is to make electric candles. I could readily imagine the scene when every house had rows and rows of actual candles, along the windowsills; along the middle sash; in straight lines, in curves, or in triangles. They were not small Christmas-tree candles but large ones like those used on church altars. Many families brought out the rare old silver candlesticks of the past for this special occasion. I can imagine how impressive Beacon Hill was in those early Christmas days when the street lamps were only dimmed kerosene lights. It must have glowed like a huge warmth-giving fireplace. The natural vibration of the real candle-lights must have created ethereal waves of yellow, red, or orange, making the scene more lively and deepening the feeling. On the other hand the gradual diminution in the length of the candle would intensify the sense of time and tantalise the emotions in that way. After all, a human being is a sentimental creature, not made only of laboratory elements.

I have been seeking information about the invention of candles for some time. As discovering how to use fire was the beginning of progress, so producing candles must have helped the development of human civilisation tremendously. This research is my personal fun. Professor L. Carrington Goodrich of Columbia University, editor of Carter's *The Invention of Printing in China and Its Spread Westward* and writer of several books and articles on the development of science in ancient China, was inclined to agree with me that candles may first have been used in China, though we have not any definite evidence for the theory yet. Excavations in China in the past forty years show that Chinese civilisation was highly developed in the Shang-Yin period about the seventeenth century B.C. Many fine bronzes have been found and some of them may have been treated to the lost wax method of casting. Wax, or *la* in Chinese, is the material for making candles. A number of early Chinese books describe how wax was collected from beehives, and the early candles in China were called beeswax candles. One book mentions a special kind of insect, really a moth, with its wings full of wax material. This insect has long been known in three provinces, Szechuan, Kweiyang and Chekiang; the natives there used to feed it with the small bushes of wax-trees, and it bred in large numbers. They gathered the wax from the wings of the insects to make candles. This wax is white in colour and it is therefore called *pai-la* in Chinese, while the beeswax is yellow wax. The Szechuan and Chekiang candles have been renowned in China for centuries. The burning of red candles in China symbolizes happiness and takes place on every happy festival occasion. I naturally had the happy association with the window candle-lights on Beacon Hill.

The eventful eve, Christmas Eve, at long last approached. Mr. MacFarlane, in whose house I was staying, informed me that it was an old Beacon Hill custom to keep open-house that evening and to have sandwiches and candy ready for Christmas bellringers and carol-singers who called. I said that my friends from Cambridge wanted to come and see Beacon Hill that evening. He kindly had the front room specially arranged for me and my friends, saying that we would be welcome to share in the sandwiches and candies. Real candles burnt cheerfully in the window of the front room and seemed to be the signal for callers. I was waiting for my friends and heard footsteps, so I went to open the door. A happy voice cried "Merry Christmas," and a tinkle of little bells filled my ears. Roaring with laughter the visitor, a middle-aged lady, held up part of her coat and gave a hard shake. The bells lined the edges of the coat and rang merrily. The lady was beautifully rouged and powdered, her hat was gay with colour, and her manner jubilant. She walked straight inside, before I could say a word; she did not seem to be startled at seeing my flat face. Soon a group of five young people came in, none of whom had any bells to ring, but all a good appetite for sandwiches. I had to take part in the meal, so I asked my friends, Professor and Mrs. Yang and their daughter, Shu-li, and son Te-cheng, together with Mr. and Mrs. Chen-huan Yui, to go to Louisburg Square for a good look first.

When I reached Louisburg Square there was hardly any standing space left. A group of bellringers, men and women, old and young, each hand holding one bell which they moved

and rang to and fro as they sang, stood in front of the door
step of a house in Louisburg Square not far from the side of
Mount Vernon Street. Many of the people standing by had
a carol sheet in their hands and joined in the singing with
the bellringers, heartily yet reverently. I heard someone say
that the bellringers had just come in from Mount Vernon

Bell-ringing and carol-singing

Street and that there were a few other groups somewhere
else on the hill. More people were streaming into the square,
and the atmosphere became warmer and gayer than before.
A boy was trying to climb up a nearby lamp-post so that he
could see the bellringers more clearly, but he was told to get
down. There must have been a large number of Harvard

students amongst those who joined in the singing, for many looked young and familiar. Presently four young men arrived in different costumes—two wearing high silk hats, one in a Scottish tartan, and the fourth dressed as a cowboy. Their appearance made all eyes bright, yet in spite of the

Rector's House of Trinity Church near Copley Square

multitude of people and the excitement, a well-behaved and highly disciplined atmosphere prevailed. I found it impressive.

I remained in the Square for some time. When the crowd thinned, I picked up a carol sheet and read one of the verses:

> O little town of Bethlehem,
> How still we see thee lie;

> Above thy deep and dreamless sleep
> The silent stars go by . . .

This I found to have been written some ninety years ago by Phillips Brooks, Bishop of Massachusetts, who was Rector of Trinity Church in Copley Square. Every Christmas Eve, on Beacon Hill, the carollers sing it to his memory.

As I made my way back to Pinckney Street, I met a few small groups still singing on their way. The windows of all the houses remained aglow and the happiness lingered on in the air. Nothing could describe it better than the following lines by Wordsworth:

> And who but listened? till was paid
>   Respect to every inmate's claim;
> The greeting given, the music played,
>   In honour of each household name,
> Duly pronounced with lusty call,
> And "Merry Christmas" wished to all.

IV

Boston Snow

I HAVE encountered deep snow in many a countryside on numerous occasions, but never before in a city. Neither London nor Paris had much snow when I was there; what snow they have in winter is only a thin, unnoticeable layer which has soon gone again. The old city of Peking is often covered with snow under the dry-cold winter sun, but as it is a big city and has many spacious streets and wide-open places, snow in Peking never appears to be unusually deep. The inhabitants take it for granted and enjoy its power to enhance the beauty of the ancient capital of China while it lasts. Snow did fall very heavily on New York in February, 1946, during my first visit, but it was made to disappear almost the next day by a whole troop of workers with many bulldozers. Not many people in New York have a good word for snow, deep or otherwise. I doubt if the majority of the inhabitants of Boston like it either. It is a nuisance for those who have to walk and also for those who have to put chains on their cars. But in Boston it was allowed to remain and I enjoyed the Boston snow while it lasted. I woke before five o'clock one morning. A brightness coming through my window made my room white. There was an unusual stillness in the air. I jumped out of bed and went straight to the window to look out:

> A night made hoary with the swarm
> And whirl-dance of the blinding storm,
> As zigzag wavering to and fro
> Crossed and recrossed the winged snow.

46

It seemed as if Whittier had written those lines specially for me at that moment. I dressed unconventionally and went downstairs stealthily for a peep at Pinckney Street. A white drift had piled high on the doorstep, and a flurry of snowflakes pushed me back. But I was undaunted and thrust my feet in the white blanket, one after the other, until I was nearly stamping up to my knee. There were a few small snow-hills in the front of some of the houses; I guessed that each concealed a motor-car. I made my way back to my room and read Whittier's poem to the end in bed.

The little book, *Snow-Bound*, published by the Trustees of the John Greenleaf Whittier Homestead, was given to me by Walter Whitehill when he took me to see Whittier's birthplace at Haverhill, the scene of which the poem describes. On our way we visited one of the trustees, Willard G. Cogswell, an eminent lawyer, who lived nearby. As well as his profound knowledge of law, Cogswell had a great love of gardens. I was delighted to find that in his garden he had made use of natural rocks for ornament as we do in China. To keep one's mind in harmony with nature is to prevent madness. Life within the bare walls of an office or a laboratory full of test tubes is not far from an asylum. A beloved home is indeed a place where man can be sane. Whittier expressed his feeling for the home he was born in and never forgot. Though the external scene has now changed much since his day, the inside of his home is preserved as it was. Though the length and metrical form of his poem are quite different from the Chinese, the inner meaning and feeling it conveys could move any one in China as it did me.

Whittier once said with reference to deep snow: "Our fathers, coming from the milder climate of England, had the traditional English slowness in adapting themselves to changed climatic conditions." This made me wonder how the first owners of the houses on Beacon Hill reacted to the deep snow they must have experienced.

On this first morning of snow in Boston I had an appointment at eleven o'clock. In order to experience the snow, I left the house at eight. Pinckney Street was not the Pinckney Street of the night before. Before I reached Louisburg Square my eyes gazed on and on over the wide stretch: "no cloud above, no earth below— A universe of sky and snow!" as Whittier put it. But the line, "no earth below" should become "no Charles River below." I seemed to look on a long, silky white carpet laid down for some royal figures to walk over in a stately procession to infinity. There was complete silence on all sides, and the street seemed unusually wide. I knew I was not expected to walk on this carpet, and quickly turned left into Louisburg Square.

The atmosphere in the Square was soft and mild—and contradicted the temperature I had read inside the house a moment ago. The red bricks glowed redder against the great whiteness of the snow as if they were modern artificial coals with electric bulbs behind them in a fireplace. The stone-carved figure of Columbus had developed an elongated body, wrapped in a cloak of white velvet; his legs and the pedestal were all lost in the snow. The oval-shaped iron-fenced enclosure in the center of the Square had become a snow-container, where none of the usual visitors—birds, squirrels, or cats—was to be seen. Birds could have flown off; cats might be curled up in the warmth of the houses; but where could the squirrels be? I raked the tree-tops with my eyes. Oh, the few tall, almost straight elms were never so beautiful as at that moment. I saw them forming a Chinese *P'ai-fang,* an honorific arch or gateway, temporarily put up for the great celebration of the seventieth birthday of Emperor K'ang Hsi in the old capital of Peking over two hundred years ago. Yet there was a difference, for each tree and each branch was encrusted with a bright and delicate layer of frost or crystallised snow, intricate as carved ivory. Lifting my head, I found the ivory lines becoming transparent along the top branches against the dull sky. I was filled with a sense of awe in the face of such simple beauty. Perhaps here was the point from which the procession would set out to go down the long, silky white carpet laid on Pinckney Street. A door creaked and I moved on to Mount Vernon Street and waited for a while. Nothing happened. Absolute silence reigned again in the Square.

On my way down Willow Street I noticed some iron railings still remaining around the walls of the houses. They had been there for the inhabitants to hold on to when going up and down Beacon Hill on slippery days in the past. They had been there, too, for people to tie the reins of their horses to. Life on Beacon Hill may have been brought to a standstill in those days by a heavy fall of snow. Nevertheless, life has gone on until the present day, it must go on, and nothing can bar its movement, neither heavy snow nor anything else. It is still Nature's gift to man that really counts—the brain that thinks and the limbs that move. This happy thought of ever-going-on life tickled my brain and moved my limbs down and down till I stopped on Beacon Street.

I had to stop while a stream of cars moved in a long chain along the snow-free center of the street. Then I crossed to the edge of Boston Common, which had become infinitely bigger than usual with every tree standing isolated, its trunk slimmer than before. Yet a moment later I could detect the busy movement of men and cars on Tremont Street right across the whole width of the Common. I saw many footprints on the Common, which showed the depth of the snow to be ten or twelve inches. Childishly I measured my feet in the moulds of others' footprints, which were always bigger. But sometimes I found no mould to fit my foot and then, led by a fanciful whim, I plunged my foot suddenly in the thick snow as if I was about to fall. The lightness of the snow and its crunchy sound helped to lift my heart, though I am not as young as at the beginning of my travels in the western world some twenty-odd years ago.

Most of the public benches were piled with snow, double or treble the thickness of the wooden slats of the seat. The strong, wide-stretching branches of the trees behind the benches, loaded with snow too, occasionally flicked down a small portion of their load which made a soft plop when it fell. I was hit on the head or shoulders as if a hidden witch or goblin high up in the trees wanted to poke fun at me. I was alone on the Common as far as I could see. In the still-ness that could almost be felt, that low, monotonous sound of the dropping snow was clearly audible without causing any disturbance. This was perhaps the nearest approach that life and nature could make to absolute silence. Suddenly the scream of an ambulance pierced my ears and I realised that I was getting near the edge of the Common.

I was now on the mound where the Army and Navy Monu-ment stands. On other days the trees grow all round the mound and enclose the Monument in a secluded place, but now it was open to view. I have encountered too many mon-uments and statues now in my travels, and they do not hold me for a look any more, for I confuse one with another, not that I have less respect for the person commemorated and for the artist who sculptured the memorial. The heavy snow that hung on the top branches of the trees that grow a little way down the mound was satisfying my eye. Instead of clear-cut ivory lines I saw round buns of pure white flour arranged in rows or scattered in no definite order, all ready for baking.

A small black figure between two tree trunks soon caught my eye. When I reached the spot, I found that an elderly fellow had cleared the snow off a bench and was sitting feeding the birds in countless numbers. There were sparrows and some starlings, but pigeons and blackbirds outnumbered them all. All the birds of the Common must have gathered here. From a distance the old fellow looked content and happy; when I got nearer I saw that he was in great difficulties. He kept moving his arms up and down and shifting his head to and fro, for all the birds wanted to perch on them. The snow was too thick on the tree branches and too deep on the ground for them. The starlings proved stronger and fiercer even than the pigeons in finding a foothold on the old fellow. In having to fly up and struggle for the crumbs, some lost their hold but soon recovered it again. There was a constant commotion in the air, a contrast from the absolute silence that I had experienced a moment ago. Apparently the old fellow had a definite idea in feeding the birds. He gave me an appealing look for sympathy and said with a grin that he only had bread enough to feed the small birds, but that he could not prevent the bigger ones gathering round him too, in spite of flapping his arms in order to push them away. Unfortunately starlings are noted for their boldness, blackbirds are fearless and frank gluttons, and pigeons are the most persistent, hard-boiled and shameless creatures among the feathered race. Each expresses its shyness to man, but in time of hunger they forget their shyness. I found no words to reply. The bird-feeder was performing a good deed, yet that good deed of his got him into great entanglement. Such is life, one side of life.

I then crossed Charles Street. Hilarious sounds filled the air of the Public Garden. There is usually a good side to things. The deep Boston snow gave a chance of vigorous and healthy outdoor exercise to Boston inhabitants, old and young. Snowballs were flying to and fro and many people were skating on the frog pond. It must have been a good skating rink, for the small surface of the pond on both sides

Skating on Frog Pond

of the bridge had become a solid piece of unbreakable ice. As they whirled, some fell at times. All laughed and shouted. I wondered how so many could be there on a Friday morning. At last the time for my appointment was getting near, and I decided to leave the enjoyment of watching the merriment on the pond to the next day.

This appointment had been made a few days before during a lunch at the Tavern Club with Dr. M. A. DeWolfe Howe. The atmosphere inside that club immediately took

me back to that of Ye Olde Cheshire Cheese off Fleet Street
near St. Paul's in London, where Dr. Samuel Johnson used
to meet his friend and talk to the parrot owned by the proprietor. Ye Olde Cheshire Cheese is only a tavern still, carrying on its restaurant business as in Johnson's day, but the
Tavern Club is one of the older clubs in Boston, with a
reading and writing room, smoking room, billiard room etc.
Seven of us had lunch at a round table: Charles Hopkinson
the noted Boston portrait painter, Samuel Chamberlain the
famous New England photographer and authority on French
and Italian cooking, Langdon Warner the expert on Far
Eastern art, with whom I had corresponded many a time
through our mutual friend, Walter Beck, but whom I had
not met before, and his friend, also a member of the club
but whose name I did not catch. The last was Erwin D.
Canham, a Rhodes scholar and editor of the *Christian Science Monitor*. I remarked that I had been reading the *Christian Science Monitor* for a few years, as my friends, Robert
and Thelma Morris of Sacramento, California, used to send
it to me in Oxford. Langdon Warner declared: "I strongly
recommend you to read the *Christian Science Monitor* here.
It is the only decent paper I read. It is a real newspaper, unlike the others, which are full of advertisements and of unpleasant accounts of social events of no importance whatso-
ever." All nodded in agreement. I must record here that
after that first lunch I came to the club twice more. One
morning I was standing opposite it, trying to make a rough
sketch of its entrance doorway. Suddenly my left arm was
seized by a tall, white-haired man, who stopped and asked
me: "Tell me, what is that little house? I have been passing
the front of it on my way to my office for the past thirty-six
years. I have seen many old men with white moustaches and
bent shoulders coming and going. All Boston learned men

I suppose. Many big men of Europe come, too. When the big man of England, Winston Churchill, arrived, this little street was full of people and I just couldn't get through. Tell me, what is that little house?" I told him it was the Tavern Club and that I had been there and there was nothing unusual inside. He laughed and continued: "You must have been the only black-headed man there. Did you enjoy being inside?" "Not 'arf" slipped out of my mouth too readily. I said this to indicate where I came from and also to show how much I know. My inquirer might have been puzzled by this London cockney's expression, "Not 'arf," but he waved happily to me when he went on his way.

Perhaps it was the fact that I had lived in Oxford which interested Mr. Canham. He arranged to show me over his publishing building at Norway Street. Neither of us could have foreseen that there would be a heavy fall of snow before we met again. The Chinese have a reputation in the West for being unpunctual for appointments. I try to contradict that reputation whenever possible. I reached my destination on time, but unfortunately I got lost inside the vastness of the Christian Science Publishing Building. A young girl clerk kindly directed me through a long corridor after I had already lost my way twice, and I eventually reached the section of the *Christian Science Monitor* a quarter of an hour late.

Mr. Canham showed me his editorial department and also the composing department, both of which are very big, involving a large number of personnel. "Before you go," said he, "I must show you our Globe Room." Presently we entered a room of unusual size and structure, ceiling and walls combining to form a sphere. When we went onto a glass platform I saw on all sides an enormous map of the world painted on glass and lit up from the other side. I remarked that I was quite used to reading a large globe map of the world from the outside but had never read one from inside before. My host smiled and explained that the architect who designed this room, known as a Mapparium, looked upon the *Christian Science Monitor* as an international paper, so installed a globe at hand. I was also told that the architect

In Globe Room

had foresight into world events and had realised that changes were possible. Mr. Canham then pointed out that a number of places on the map needed to be changed but added that there had been no time to do this yet. Later our conversation concerned the scarcity of land on the map in view of the ever-increasing population of the world. I had never realised that there was so much water.

When I came out, I realised that I had gone in by the wrong entrance. The mistake was fruitful, for otherwise I would not have seen the department which publishes Mrs. Eddy's works nor the size of the whole building. It is magnificent to look at from outside, though the snow prevented me seeing it from every angle. Following the direction given to me by Mr. Canham, I crossed the snow to the First Church of Christ Scientist, or "The Mother Church," as it is called. There is no altarpiece with statues, flowers, and a Cross, as I have seen in other churches. All the seats are made of pear-wood and varnished yellowish brown. The window colours seemed to match that of the seats very well, for the window-glass was only light blue, green, and yellow with very little red, unlike traditional stained glass which is mostly in long narrow windows with deep red, purple, and royal blue as chief colours. The traditional stained glass aims at intensify-ing the awe of those who come to worship, but this Mother Church, with lighter colouring and no deep red and purple colours for its windows, must create a soothing calm in the mind by its mellow warmth. The original part of the old church was shown to me. It is kept as it was in Mrs. Eddy's day.

Leaving the Mother Church, I walked a little distance on Falmouth Street to have a look at it as a whole. The old square tower and the old part of the church blend together splendidly. The big dome, I was told, is twice as big as that of the State House on Beacon Hill and higher than Bunker Hill Monument. Much of the church was heavily capped with snow, and the firm, solid stance of the whole building was particularly emphasized by the great whiteness that sur-rounded it. It signified to me that other stormy days it had witnessed in the past had all added to its solidity and firm-ness. I made a quick sketch of it before I moved down the garden for another look from a different angle.

I did not go back the same way as I had come, by the Huntington Avenue car, for I knew that I was not far from the Fens. The snow began to fall heavily again when I was walking through the Fenway. I found a path made by some who had walked before me. The vast, pure white carpet of the snow helped me to think more clearly than indoors or inside a car. I moved on, despite the flying flakes that beat against my face. I was thinking that Christian Science is a branch growing out of the original Christianity. It had a difficult start; it met wind and rain; it took root and has flourished far and wide, within a number of years that one could count easily. Mrs. Eddy launched Christian Science only about three-quarters of a century ago. A new branch of an old religion, or say a new religion in itself springing up within living memory, is altogether unbelievable, for all the religions of the world we know are full of antiquity and many things about them we simply could not know. For instance, I have myself long been interested in Chinese Ch'an Buddhism (the Japanese word *Zen* is now the more widely known term for the sect), which branched off from Indian Buddhism and established itself in China in the sixth century. But I cannot say anything definite about its early history or its first founder. I doubt if any other religion has as clear and recent a history as Christian Science.

I have been to the publishing quarters of the *London Times* and have also seen the *New York Times* building in Times Square. Though both *Times*es can be bought in other countries, they aim their sales chiefly at their own. Only the *Christian Science Monitor* aims to be sold in all parts of the world—at least, some of its articles are printed in the major European languages, including Russian. Indeed, Boston has enriched my mind with information about the beginning of the history of a nation, the establishing of a new religion, and the publication of a daily paper that circulates throughout the world.

Presently I lifted my head and found the snow flakes becoming even thicker, veiling all objects, near and far, from my sight. I was cheerfully walking in the world of the past, yet still in the present, and on the way to coming days.

Snow over Boston Common

Snow falls continually;
Few people walk.
Before my eyes a shroud of white dazzles
    and confuses the scene.
In the distant trees there seems
    liveliness.
Flocks of birds cry noisily,
    snatching crumbs;
Big and small,
Hungry every one.

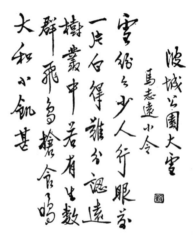

V

Boston Palace

H A S B O S T O N a Palace? Historical as Boston is, it has never been the capital of the U.S.A. nor is America headed by a king or an emperor residing inside a luxurious palace in the old Oriental or European style. Nevertheless, there is a palace in Boston. It is Fenway Court.

Through the kind introduction of the Misses Frances and Norvelle Browne of New York, I had an invitation from the director of Fenway Court to see it. In my unchangeable manner I reached Fenway open ground early to have a stroll first. The Boston Museum of Fine Arts has a Fenway façade. I had a good look at its clear reflection in the pond and then moved to the rose garden where the gardeners had every plant covered up for winter. Ducks, even in cold January, were playing under a wooden bridge. I chuckled to myself, remembering a quarrel between two Chinese poets. Mao Ta-k'o of the eighteenth century had never a good word to say for the poetry of Su Tung-p'o of the eleventh century, whose poetic works have otherwise won all Chinese hearts. One day a friend visited Mao and they began to have a heated argument on this point. "At least," said the friend, "you can have no quarrel with Su's 'Lines in Springtime':

Through the bamboo-grove peach blossoms peer—two or three
    branches;
Spring water is warm in the stream,—ducks know it first.

Could anything be more charming?"

"Pooh!" replied Mao, in deep scorn, "it is not even accurate; why, the geese are just as quick as ducks about things like that—that man with his everlasting ducks . . ."

This sounds as if Mao Ta-k'o would have been able to lead

Kuan Yin slips out of the Boston Museum for meditation

a successful life in this modern age of ours if he came to live in America. I presume in the light of Chinese Taoism, which declares every creature in Nature to be as sensitive as any human being, that ducks do possess knowledge. Involuntarily I asked myself if the ducks on the Fenway stream knew about their proud ancestors, who must have witnessed many interesting processions of noted personalities in and out of Fenway Court half a century ago. Is there a Duck Genealogical Society in Boston, where the baby ducklings, when grown up, go to find out the names of their ancestors? Suddenly some big raindrops disturbed the surface of the water and one duck broke into quacking, followed by two others. They were no doubt answering my questions in their language, but I could not understand. So I crossed the road.

Mr. Morris Carter, Director of Fenway Court, received me with a broad smile, saying "You are just the man I have been

Ducks in Fenway Lake

waiting for." Before I could apologise for keeping him waiting, I was led through the corridor and asked to sit on the stone bench facing the central courtyard. This courtyard would be called in Chinese *T'ien Ching*, or *sky-well*, for it is surrounded by high walls on four sides, with an open top to allow the light to brighten the rooms through the windows. My old home in Kiukiang, China, had three sky-wells similar to this, though no cloisters and a different window structure. From where I was sitting I observed the old look and the purplish colour of the walls, and assumed the building to be unusual in Boston or even in the whole U.S.A. All the windows wear their Italian Renaissance decorations. The stone steps leading to the cloisters from the courtyard on each side suggested Europe.

"When Mrs. Gardner returned to Boston from Europe in December, 1899," my host told me with a smile, "a newspaper announced that she had bought an Italian palace and would ship it to Boston and set it up as an art memorial to her husband; it was a Florentine palace, built during the Renaissance when Florentine architecture was at its height, and the article said that those who knew the Pitti Palace would be able to imagine the type Mrs. Gardner had bought." I was then told of the difficulties Mrs. Gardner encountered before it was reconstructed in Boston, and of the endless pains she took in supervising the work herself. She even helped the workmen to mix the pigments and to get the mellow colour correct for the walls, and took meals with them as if she was one of them on the job. The palace created an enormous sensation when it was finished and opened. Exciting parties were held in it. Contemporary writers, musicians, poets, and painters seem to have surrounded Mrs. Gardner as if she were a queen. I have read and heard how many a palace was designed and built by a king or an emperor in Europe and Asia, but none was so dramatic nor had such glamour as this one, built at the beginning of the present century. Yet it was a mere transplantation. The place where Fenway Court was originally situated in Italy was never mentioned. How this idea of removing a palace from one continent to another came to be conceived is beyond my comprehension. Years ago in Shanghai, I saw a movie entitled *The Ghost Goes West*, in which a Scottish castle was bought by an American descendant and removed brick by brick to be rebuilt in America, but the

ghost of the Scottish ancestor made its way to America too
and ruled over the family. I wonder if the ancient owner of
Fenway Court ever came along!

Fenway Court has developed one original feature in its
new setting. This is the beautiful arrangement of flowers in
the center and corners of the courtyard. I do not mean that
there are no flower arrangements in the courtyard of an
Italian palace, but I cannot recall any. Here were flowers
in great variety—paying tribute to Mrs. Gardner's fine
taste, for the arrangement still continued in the tradition
she established and all the flowers are home-grown.

I do not know how our talk turned to Mrs. Gardner's
family. Mr. Carter said with a happy smile that pride of race
has always flourished in Boston and that Mrs. Gardner's simple statement was that she was descended from Robert Bruce
of Scotland and counted Mary Stewart among her ancestors.
She actually belonged to the Invernahyle branch of the Ap-
pin Stewarts. She was not a Bostonian, yet she left Boston
a palace.

We then moved slowly through the Chapel, the Dutch
Room, the Tapestry Room, the Gothic Room, and the
Music Room, while a number of important art objects were
pointed out to me on our way. I was particularly interested
in seeing a Chinese pair of bronze bears—very rare. Every
object is displayed and every piece of furniture stands strictly
where it used to be in Mrs. Gardner's days, according to the
terms of her will. The living rooms on the top of the building are now occupied by the director and his family.

After a while I was left to wander round on my own. I
found my way to Sargent's portrait of Mrs. Gardner and
also his "El Jaleo." I then joined Mr. Carter in the Music
Room, to listen to a concert which was the event of that particular afternoon. A young soprano named Jane Schleicher

sang twice, drawing much applause from the audience.

Some weeks later, the Carters gave a dinner party in the top rooms of Fenway Court at which I was privileged to be present. I was seated on the right of our hostess, while our mutual friend, Mrs. George Bemis, was on the right of our host. A group of beautiful large Mexican orchids in a purple glass bowl to match them were reflected in the spotless, lacquered surface of the long dining table. Someone admired the elegant and fine dinner set. Mrs. Carter remarked that that was the set Mrs. Gardner had brought back from Italy and had often used for special parties. The last time it had been used was at a dinner for the Archbishop of Canterbury, Dr. Fisher of Great Britain, in 1952. While we were enjoying delicious food and congenial company and conversing happily, a soft tune suddenly started somewhere outside the hall and gradually came more loudly through the cracks of the windows. It halted our conversation, and we rose from our seats to go to the windows, which Mr. Carter opened.

The light was somewhat dimmed in the courtyard, giving a bluish hue to purplish walls, yet it was as fresh and clear as full moonlight. The softly outlined silhouette of a singer showed behind the Venetian window and his song, carried on ethereal waves of sound, created an exotic atmosphere that transplanted all of us to a scene unreal yet tranquilly alive. The song, though unintelligible to my ears, was very agreeable and soothing, sometimes far, far away and sometimes near at hand. It seemed as if it were being sung by a gondolier or someone in the higher story of a house by the waterway of Venice while our boat drifted on and on. We were moving quietly and slowly from one room to another, while the gentle voices among us, almost whispering, sounded like the chirping noise of the sparrows in the bushes under the spell of a skylark in the air. We were all in evening dress. The trailing of the ladies' gowns—a wonderful invention for gracefulness—set the leisurely pace for us men. We moved on inch by inch as if we were in a procession, while the echo of the song became fainter and fainter.

Boston palace

Presently we reached the elevator, which carried a full load of ladies to the ground, while we men walked down the spiral staircase. We came back to earth—in Boston. All of us gesticulated like a flock of children out of a class from a coeducational school. Admiration and appreciation were idly exchanged, and our hostess nodded her head smilingly. I learnt that the singer was Mr. Wesley Copperstone, a noted tenor in the city.

Mr. Carter led the procession round the cloisters. The moonlight effect became paler, as if a sheet of frost had covered all the plants in the courtyard. Chilliness permeated the air. Our gaiety was more restrained than when we were upstairs, for the cold atmosphere put an end to the chirping of the ladies, and the skylark had long disappeared. The soft movement of our footsteps sounded clearly now and then as we proceeded through the cloisters to the family Chapel. The big canvas of Sargent's "El Jaleo" was lit up for us. There was no other light. We continued to move very slowly through a dark corridor where by degrees we could not even distinguish the walls. My eyes closed for a moment. Someone must have shivered, causing her satin dress to produce a gentle noise. All of a sudden, two huge doors flew wide open. Straight in front of us, a big fire was blazing and crackling in an enormous fireplace. Our eyes opened wide but were soon blinded by the dazzling brightness after the pitch darkness a moment before. I had to close mine again for a moment. Soon we were all seated in astonishment or stood staring at the fire open-mouthed. Nothing could have been more appreciated than its warmth after the chilly night air nor more dramatic than the way it burst upon us. Our host had planned this, perhaps in Mrs. Gardner's tradition. We were still commenting on the sudden appearance of the blazing fire while we were bidding the Carters goodnight.

Eleanor Early wrote: "For years and years Mrs. Jack Gardner scandalized society. She was reckless, witty, and gay. Not a pretty woman, but a fascinating one, with curves, and red hair, and arms that artists loved to paint. In the early eighties Boston was rather a provincial city, and life was simple. Boston's jaw dropped—Boston's eyes bulged—when Mrs. Gardner drove out with *three* liveried men on her carriage. Her dresses were lovelier than any one else's. Her jewels brighter. And her stories naughtier. She had two enormous diamonds named 'The Rajah' and 'The Light of India,' set on springs so that they waved above her forehead like antennae. And she wore her pearls around her waist, instead of her neck. . . .

"No woman in society was ever so maligned as Mrs. Jack Gardner. She had a penchant for gifted youths. Under her eye they developed into artists, novelists, poets, and geniuses of all sorts. And, naturally, they danced attendance upon her and sang her praises day and night. Which made all the other ladies jealous."

I took a good look at her curves, red hair, and arms in Sargent's portrait of her. In *Sargent's Boston* my friend, David McKibbin says, "Mrs. Gardner, at the time of Sargent's 1887–88 visit to Boston, was living at 152 Beacon Street. . . . In October, 1886, Henry James and Ralph Curtis took her to Sargent's studio in London to see the already famous portrait of Madame Gautreau. With the recollection of this in mind, Mrs. Gardner asked Sargent to paint her portrait while he was in Boston. It proved a formidable assignment, for the first eight attempts failed. When the ninth succeeded, the portrait was declared by Mrs. Gardner to be the finest Sargent ever painted." Unfortunately there is no record of the artist's own opinion. Sargent was already a most noted portrait-painter in England and America. Mrs. Gardner must have had an unwavering idea about how her curves, red hair, and arms should be painted. Indeed, Mrs. Gardner was a fascinating woman.

I learnt that she was an ardent believer in the maintenance of native customs, native costumes, native ceremonies, and native religions. She found Oriental religious rites picturesque and interesting. When she grew older she regretted the gradual Europeanization of Asia, the destruction of variety, the increasing uniformity and monotony in the way of life. Once when a distinguished Japanese came to Boston, she declined the honour of receiving him in Fenway Court because he wore European clothes; she liked to have her Japanese friends in her box at the opera, but they clearly understood that they would not be welcome unless they came in Japanese costume. I feel glad in a way that I did not come to see Boston in her day, for the few Chinese dresses I brought over when I came to England some twenty odd years ago are nearly all worn out and it has been very difficult to replace them. She might have known that the laundrymen in America would not willingly accept unusual types of costume for cleaning.

Apart from its wonderful art treasures, Fenway Court has excited people since its construction and will excite generations to come simply because it is a Venetian Palace in Boston.

Once, in London, I heard Verdi's opera *A Masked Ball* in Covent Garden Theatre, London, and was interested to read afterwards an article by Cecil Smith in which he stated: "To a New Englander, everything is wrong with this plot," and went on to say that to get around the objection of a Roman censor in 1859, Verdi had transplanted his story from Rome to a fictional Boston.

A palace in Boston sounds fictional. Yet Fenway Court is one!

Rose Garden in Fenway

Charming is spring at its height!
Roses vie in beauty with one another.
Such a fine day seems to intoxicate me.
Pairs of swallows dart like flying arrows.

The Fenway Rose Garden

Church of The Advent
and Charles Street Universalist Meeting House

An idle moment in busy living;
I stroll leisurely, smiling
At the myriad senses of life!

苔微玫瑰園
春閨怨

婷妮春深薔薇鬥
貂看來欲醉好晴
天雙～燕子飛々
等忙裡閑漫步閑
新生々意萬千

VI

Boston Water

THE CHARLES RIVER was the first Boston water I saw.
It is as conspicuous in Boston as Beacon Hill. The Charles
River was a river before it got its name, "Charles," and is
still a river more than three hundred years after the found-
ing of Boston. Boston friends insist on telling me that by
the Charles River lived the makers of America and that the
bridge known as "The Great Bridge" across the Charles to
Cambridge, opened for use in 1662, was the *first* bridge of
any importance built in America. I was also told that the
Algonquin Indians, who lived in this neighbourhood before
the Bostonians, called the river "Quineboquin," meaning
twisting or *circular,* for the river has many curves and turns
in its sixty-mile course from Echo Lake by the town of Hopkinton. More names make me more confused. Casually I
enquired why and when it was named the "Charles." A smile
was the only response.

Very soon after I came to live in Pinckney Street I got up
one morning earlier than usual in the hope of tasting the
subtle sensation of walking down a hill inside a big city. To
step down Beacon Hill was unlike going down a tree-covered
hill, for there were no trees along Pinckney Street. Nevertheless, the air was fresher than on the flat ground, I felt, and
the view in the distance was alluring beyond the end of a
long, bright skiing path lined with houses instead of trees.
Gradually the white Greek-temple-like buildings of the
Massachusetts Institute of Technology came to view and
they soon gleamed in the sunlight. It was a wonder to me to

see the sky so blue at this early hour of the day after my years of residence by the Thames. I soon sat down on a bench close to the river's edge. From there the water surface did not look as calm as from the hill a moment ago. The wind was whistling through the tree leaves behind me. The rip-

Morning activities on the Charles

ples or waves were pushing each other along as if they might be missing something. The Charles is a lively river.

The whistling wind brought to me the quacking of a number of ducks, swimming against the waves from the small island towards the shore where I was sitting. Did they see me from their home on the island? Or had they sensed my presence from thus far? There are many mysteries in Nature about which we can only guess. The ducks came for food; they did not know that I had not brought them any. When they discovered that they had guessed wrongly they swam on. I followed them on the shore and came to a wooden structure, on which two boys were busy. One was fishing with a short home-made rod and the younger one was sprawling on the planks, shouting with outstretched arm, "There, over there," to which came the echo, "Where? Where?" I soon noticed what they were trying to catch—a small tortoise clinging to a stone bank battered by the water but never washed off. The presence of the two boys here at such an early hour puzzled me a while. They paid no attention to

the ducks which in turn swam on without heeding them.

Such was my first stroll by the Charles. The Storrow Memorial Embankment saw me strolling by on many an occasion at different hours of the day and in different kinds of weather. I was there when some parts of the Storrow Memorial Embankment were still under construction. I stepped on one stone and then another in order to have a closer view of the ducklings taking lessons from their mother. I saw an enchanting view of Beacon Hill and the Charles from the newly-built little bridge with several weeping willows clustering in the morning mist which lent a softened tone to the whole scene. I once sat by a young willow watching a flock of ducks flying over in the direction of the Longfellow Bridge, while the long slender branches brushed my face in the gentle breeze. A glorious sunset over Boston is best seen from the shore of the Charles, for the mellowness of the red-brick houses of the city vies with it in friendly fashion.

There are always people walking along the embankment, but more round the Concert Shell on its north side than on the west. I was amazed to hear more languages spoken there then anywhere, though when I tried hard to make out what I could hear, I realised that everyone was talking English in different accents or dialects.

Fortunately or unfortunately the modern invention of radio and the circulation of newspapers have helped to eliminate differences in the New England rural dialects since the Higginson, Whittier, and Lowell days. I doubt if the fishers' wives of Marblehead still speak in the way Whittier recorded. China has been confronted with the problems of the differences in the dialects of the Chinese language for many years, and many have attempted to reform the language by adopting Roman syllables and spelling. But no reform can have any lasting effect unless the original ideograph of the Chinese written language is completely wiped out. The only way to eliminate Chinese dialects is to increase the use of the radio in teaching, and the circulation of newsprint.

Thomas Wentworth Higginson remarked that the appearance of seals under the bridge, on which he and Lowell were walking, was not uncommon in the eighteen-forties. It is obvious that Boston was then still a sort of small peninsula and the Charles wider when it joined the sea. Perhaps this accounts for the near nonexistence of fishermen along the Charles of Boston, like those fishermen along the Seine in Paris—there are no small fish for them to catch at any hour of the day.

To walk from Harvard Square to Boston for lectures seems to be an impossibility, or at least a thing that no one would attempt to do nowadays. Yet Higginson and Lowell did it many a time. Even thirty or forty years ago everyone took walking as a matter of course. Mr. Julian Claff, a graduate of Boston University, told me that he always walked the few miles from his home to college in the morning. He once even walked with a friend the fifty miles from Boston to Worcester and reached there in the evening, having walked almost incessantly for twelve hours. In his early days he and his classmates really enjoyed walking, in which there was always some unexpected fun on the way. "It is a pity," remarked Claff, "that young men of today have all learned how to drive an automobile but lost the art of walking." He also talked of the joy of walking around different parts of Paris when he worked in the Paris office of the *New York Times*. Now he cannot find time to walk, for he is so occupied with his bookselling business. "Time was plenty in the past," continued Claff with a humourous twist at the corner of his lips, "We don't have any now. Where has time gone and what have we done with it?" We both agreed not to say any more about time.

The bridge that Higginson walked over with Lowell must be the bridge about which Longfellow wrote his poem. That bridge was the predecessor of the Longfellow Bridge, so named after the famous poem, I learned. It is difficult to imagine how the scene and view looked when Higginson, Lowell, and Longfellow knew it. But the great expanse of water which used to be called "the Back Bay" is now a fine section of residential houses on the reclaimed land still called Back Bay. Since then the Charles River Dam was built and there are no more tidal waves to be seen.

Once I was caught on Harvard Bridge in a very heavy storm not long after my return from a voyage in the *Sunbeam* along the coast of Maine. My experience on board seemed to be repeating itself. The *Sunbeam* is a small boat owned by the Maine Seacoast Mission, and Rev. Neal D. Bousfield, who was born in China, and Dr. Tertius Van Dyke of Hartford Seminary took me on their voyage. We sailed with only six people on board from Seal Harbor in the early morning

in cloudy weather and poor visibility. It was raining hard,
too. About noontime the clouds lifted and I saw that the
sea along the coast of Maine could be very rough in the beginning of December. Though I was used to travel on ocean
liners, this was the first time I had been on board a small

The Sunbeam in the storm

boat in a rough sea. Captain Parry was kind enough to ask
me to enjoy a grand view from his piloting quarter. I got
out of the cabin and climbed a short ladder holding fast to
the railing while the boat rocked and the heavy raindrops
beat on my back. Captain Parry had a job to open the door,
and when it was opened I was blown in by the strong wind.
I was welcomed with a nod of the head and a happy smile
by my host who still fixed his eyes straight ahead on the sea.
His "You are a good sailor, I see," brought from me: "Well,
I have been travelling on the sea on and off for the past
twenty-five years." Many different birds flying close to the
water were pointed out to me, but I could hardly distinguish
them from a distance. When I did spot them, they soon
disappeared again in the sea as our boat was lifted high on

the tip of a wave; they were out of sight above me when we dipped. I stood by the Captain for a while and presently I just made no attempt to see what he pointed out, for I was beginning to realise that I was not a good sailor after all. I managed to climb down through the storm to the cabin

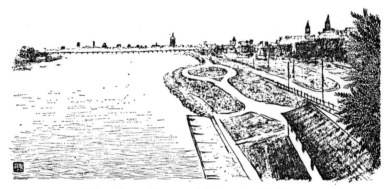

View from Boston University Bridge

with a feeling of relief but disgraced as a sailor. I vowed to myself that I should never boast. After the storm the rest of the voyage was most enjoyable and we stepped ashore on the remotest island, Matinicus, which was covered with snow. It was too soon to be reminded of that storm experience. The storm on Harvard bridge took me by surprise when I was in the middle of the path gazing at the distant view. The houses on both sides soon disappeared in the thick lines of rain and I clung to the railing of the bridge as I had clung to the railing of the *Sunbeam*. The ripples on the surface of the Charles were blown as big as the waves along the Maine coast in the storm. This dramatic scene I witnessed on the Charles in Boston could not have happened on the Thames of London, nor on the Seine of Paris.

However, the storm on the Charles did not repeat itself during my stay. I had many sunny days in Boston in six months, more than I could have had in London and Oxford in a year or two. It was on Longfellow Bridge that I discovered why the dome of the Boston State House is gilded. On a sunny day the distant view of Beacon Hill from the bridge was always hazy and no clear lines betrayed which building was which. Yet the dome of the State House could be easily detected, for its gilded face shone through the haze, although elusively. The dome seemed to move about as well, for its reflection mingled with the golden sparkles in the water of the Charles. When the sun was setting, the scene became lovelier. The gold-lined cloud-balls in the sky seemed to vie in brilliance with the dome and their reflection in the Charles in friendly contest. The red-brick walls of Boston houses breathed their mellow, purplish hue upwards to meet the downward rays of the setting sun. Nowhere, all at the same moment, had I seen a blend of colours in such harmony before. It was better still on an early autumn afternoon in the third week of September, 1953, when I came out from the Exeter Theatre and made my way straight on to Harvard bridge. I saw showers of gold leaves fluttering in the air between the golden-streaked sky and the golden ripples of the Charles, while Beacon Hill was glowing in the reddish vapour from the red-brick walls of the houses. Boston was at its best then, and I have so far found no other city capable of offering such a magnificent golden glamour.

I went with the Yang family on a small steamboat called *Flo and Ruby* for a river trip to Watertown. My two young friends, Shu-li and Te-cheng, did not seem to enjoy the wind and raindrops which were blown on their faces, and it was quite cold. But I was glad to see the towers of Lowell House, Eliot House, and others from the river. They seemed to move by for us to view, one after another. The building that interested me most on the whole trip was the tower of the Perkins

Institute and Massachusetts School for the Blind, which looked like that of the Riverside Church in Manhattan, New York, standing some distance away from the Charles. It is not the architecture of the building which interests me but the fact that it is another type of institution which was established in Boston earlier than anywhere else in the world. When Dr. Samuel Gridley Howe made his annual report in its first year 1839 he said: "This is certain, that when audiences in England and Scotland were uttering by shouts their astonishment and pleasure that blind children could read books in raised letters, it had ceased altogether to be a matter of surprise in this country, so common had it become." Under Dr. Howe's care and sympathy, the deaf, dumb, and blind child, Laura Bridgman of New Hampshire, later enjoyed an intelligent womanhood. The great work has been continued and also glorified by another miracle that happened there, for Mrs. Edward Cunningham told me that at the Perkins Institute, which bears her family name, the famous Helen Keller was educated. I had tea with Helen Keller and her companion, Miss Dorothy Thomson through the kind introduction of my friends, Gladys and Van Wyck Brooks. After tea Miss Keller moved her right hand all over my face, as she did to many others. Her knowledge of China was profound. She was about to go to Japan at the invitation of the Japanese Government. She said that she wished she could pay China a visit.

Boston's waterfront had its busiest days before Atlantic Avenue was built. But it looked to me still very busy when I reached Atlantic Avenue from Faneuil Hall through Market Street. I am in no position to compare the commerce of Boston with that of other big cities of the United States, but Atlantic Avenue has the same look and atmosphere as South Street of New York. I do not think many visitors would come this way.

I did so because I wanted to see T-Wharf and L Street. T-Wharf was pointed out to me as having been the greatest fish pier in the world some forty or fifty years ago. I saw a group of fishing boats tied together in a row and three fishermen busy with their nets. Otherwise it was very quiet in com-

T-Wharf

parison with Fishermen's Wharf in San Francisco, where there is a constant commotion day and night. Few seagulls came to T-Wharf when I was there. There was no fishy smell to attract them. Nevertheless, T-Wharf has gained its own distinction within the past forty years from the Blue Ship Tearoom, which is said to have twenty-seven windows looking across the sea. The long building which joins the tearoom has a number of projecting balconies in front of the windows of the two top storys. On those balconies I saw bearded and nonbearded men painting or gazing at the sea, and ladies stretching their legs over the railings for dancing exercise. The sound of a piano reached my ear sometimes while I walked around the pier. I was interested that Boston had taken the place of London in two movies. Unmistakably, Boston is still English in many aspects.

On a Thursday afternoon in January, 1953, I went along T-Wharf again. This time Arthur Walworth, author of the two-volume *Woodrow Wilson,* came too. The air was hazy, and it began to turn dark. We looked at the tower of the Custom House silhouetted against the sunset as if it was cut out of dark purplish paper and pasted on a soft woollen blanket of pink, yellow, blue, black, and white all fused together. There were no other people on the pier. We were the only visitors for tea in the Blue Ship Tearoom. Mrs. Howe, a niece of the first proprietress of some thirty years ago, served us tea. While we were waiting, she said that her husband would like to play some music for us. I gasped, and then noticed on the printed menu, "Mr. Russell Blake Howe, concert pianist, plays only the finest music for the guests, when not busy with his teaching; Chopin and Liszt are favorites." Walworth suggested "The Ocean," and we listened and relaxed. I asked why the tearoom was called "Blue Ship." Someone inside the kitchen explained that blue was the favorite colour of the first proprietress and that the tearoom was shaped like a ship. We later looked through a window across the sea. Dusk had fallen and nothing was really clear. Yet there was a magic in the air which seemed to exert its spell upon my imagination. The shadow of the great change that accompanied the passage of the sunset was furtive and mysterious. The whitecaps pushed each other on their way into obscurity. Though dark and calm, much was in action. I thought the moon might come up to show us what was going on. There wouldn't be any moon that evening, we

were informed. Walworth then pointed to a distant black
mound on the sea. That was the little island called Nix's Mate,
or Apple Island. On the island there used to be a gibbet. Pirates were hung on it and their bodies were buried in the
sand. The skeletons of the ringleaders were usually left as a
warning to sailors. Pirates used to lie in wait outside Boston
Bay for the white sails of Yankee ships hurrying back with
spice and gold from a trip abroad. I remarked that the word
pirate had almost lost its significance nowadays. It is the same
with the word *bandits.* Will there be anyone similar to a pirate
or bandit in the air? What can he be called? I do not think a
term need be created. This world of ours has become saner despite the constant grumpiness and quarrelsomeness of human
nature.

I heard that the local people of L Street, nicknamed
Brownies, go swimming in the sea all the year round. I reached
the beach on a windy morning. The wind blew so hard as to
prevent me getting near the sea. A solemn figure—a black dot
—stood in the water like an undaunted pole being battered
by the waves and wind. Then he came in to the shore and
stood like "Meditation by the Sea." The Brownie does live up
to his name. I then went into the aquarium for a look but
found very little to be looked at except a small boy and girl
arguing about the length of a reptile. I thought I could see the
Boston waterfront as a whole from the sea-end of Marine Park.
It was not possible, for Boston Harbor was hidden far away
behind the heavily-blown willows.

No point on the northern side of Boston gave me a stand to
have a general view of Boston Harbor either. So I decided to
take a steamer trip to Provincetown, just to see Boston from
the sea at the beginning of the voyage. I never guessed that so
many people would have the same idea, but they soon revealed
that they were not on board to look at Boston Harbor. Selling

of drinks and cocktails had already begun, and music filled the cabin. It was not a very sunny afternoon but quite windy and chilly, as a Boston August can be. I leant on the railing and watched the harbor gradually taking shape in full view as the boat moved slowly away from it. It offered me no such startling sensation as did the harbor around Lower Manhattan when I saw it for the first time, nor had it the look of Glasgow or Liverpool harbor, which are always sealed in fog. The tallest building is the tower of the Custom House, which is always the symbol of a harbor town in Europe, particularly in the British Isles. The many little islands in the harbor seemed to be guarding the city. Each was panting with white foam as if hurrying to make way for our boat to go by. While the view of Boston was diminishing to nothing, we never lost sight of land. Cape Cod was curling around Boston Bay like a fishing-hook. At times I could not see the land that was there, for I was absurdly under the spell of the sea. I was born far inland in China, and had no idea of the sea in my childhood and youth. Now I am used to the sight of the sea. After a few months' stay on Beacon Hill this voyage created an indescrib-able joy within me, simply because I was on the sea. "The sea" . . . the very words cast a spell on me as they would on seafaring people. "The sky, and shore, and cloud, and waste, and sea" elated me as we moved to the rhythm of the water.

Provincetown held me for two days. I listened to several sea-captain-looking captains telling of their adventures at sea, and I watched the old town crier going in and out of the town hall in the attire and cap of his predecessor of Pilgrim days. I made acquaintance with the Italian-campanile structure of the Pilgrim Memorial Monument, and found the name of every state engraved on its stones when I climbed to the top of it. But I was soon blown downwards. I followed a bushy-

bearded artist who wanted to show a number of us Eugene
O'Neill's summer house. Some of the party dropped out on
the way, tired of struggling through the sand. We heard that
O'Neill had to dig his house out of the drifted sand each time
he came. "Sand" is a lively element in Provincetown.

On the bus from Provincetown to Falmouth I tried to get
a glimpse of what has been described by Henry Thoreau:
"The great number of windows in the ends of the houses, and
their irregularity in size and position, here and elsewhere on
the Cape, struck us agreeably—as if each of the various occupants who had their *cunabula* behind had punched a hole
where his necessities required it and according to his size
and stature, without regard to outside effect." I was not
successful. Henry Beston had told me about his "Outermost
House" when I stayed with him at his Chimney Farm in
Nobleboro, Maine, before giving me a copy of his book to
read. This too will have to wait for my next visit to the
neighbourhood. When I reached Woods Hole, Mr. Allen W.
Clowes met me and took me in his car to have a look at the
Marine Biological Laboratory where he was working. His
mother then kindly treated me to a good lunch before I was
taken around their lovely garden by the sea. After we had
had a look at the Nobska Lighthouse, Allen saw me off for
Martha's Vineyard.

I remained on Oak Bluffs for three nights and then landed
on Nantucket for four days.

One good point about Nantucket is that no advertising bill
or board of any kind is to be seen anywhere. This is the local
law of the islanders. A number of small but neat grey-shingled
houses built in the eighteenth century by the fishing folk are
still intact and well-cared-for. The guide thought I might be
the only Chinese to have visited Nantucket. I took myself
wherever I could on foot or by coach. The dome of the old

watch tower was gilded like that of Boston State House, but it was not so conspicuous, for it is of course smaller, and it is always hidden behind trees from eye level, although I expect its golden rays pierce through the fog for the ships to see from a distance.

Gay Head

There was a bell, cast in Lisbon, Portugal, more than one hundred and fifty years ago, which rang three times in a day for some hundred and thirty-five years, each time fifty-two strokes. When I asked why fifty-two I was jokingly told that there are fifty-two playing cards in a pack, as a Quaker town should know! Some one remarked that the English navigator, Bartholomew Gosnold, first came to Nantucket in 1602; others said that the island really belonged to the "Portygees" as their fishermen came freely for hundreds of years.

One thing on Nantucket I had to postpone seeing until another time. It was the "Hidden Forest" that a New York friend had told me about. She said that the existence of this

place was unknown to many people even on Nantucket. A
relative of hers lived near it, but had never been there, until
she suggested a visit. They set out by car but at a stile had
to get out and walk. They walked along a narrow path on
and on for a long while without seeing any forest. They were
disappointed and discouraged. Suddenly the narrow path
led into an open space with huge beech trees here and there.
Owing to the strong wind blowing from the ocean, the trees,
though stout and strong, could not grow upwards but had
to turn sideways; therefore their thick and heavy branches
twisted and interlocked—somewhat like the trees in Arthur
Rackham's or Edmund Dulac's illustrations of fairy tales—
to form a roof, underneath which the solid tree-trunks looked
like huge pillars. It was awe-inspiring to walk through, but
the Forest seemed to have no end, so they turned back home
after a half-an-hour. She strongly believed that there must be
fairies in other parts of the Hidden Forest where they did
not manage to go, and suggested that I should try to get a
glimpse of the Forest when I was on Nantucket. I did slip
away from the rest of the party when we all got out of the
coach near the Sankaty Head Light House. While all were
eagerly running over the sand and exclaiming at its depth,
I spotted a big stretch of green away from the beach and
went straight towards it. It turned out to be not grass on
the sand-dunes but the thick foliage of bushes and trees,
the trunks of which were hidden underneath. I tried to
locate a passable path but it was impossible, for the growth
was so thick and the small branches were not only interlocked
but covered by mud and sand. Eventually I found an opening and went slowly down with only my head at ground
level. But shouts from the coach were blown to my ears and I
had no alternative but to rejoin the company and return to
the center of the island. I had never wished more that I

owned a car.

On the way back my thought turned to the following famous story of "Peach Blossom Fountain" by T'ao Chien, the fourth-century poet born near Kiukiang where I was born:

In the reign of T'ai-yüan (376–396) of Chin dynasty, a man of Wu-ling took fishing for his profession and, one day, lost his way among the creeks of a river, and came upon a dense and lovely grove of peach-trees in full bloom, through which he pushed his boat, anxious to see how far the grove extended. Eventually the peach-trees ended where the water began, at the foot of a hill. He soon espied what seemed to be a small cave, from which issued light. So he fastened his boat to a tree and crept in through the narrow entrance, which shortly ushered him into a new world of level country, of fine houses, of rich fields, of fine pools, and luxuriance of bamboo and mulberry. Big roads ran north and south with noises of dogs barking and cocks crowing around. The attire of the people who came and went on the roads and to the fields was different from what he knew. Both young and old appeared to be happy and contented. When someone spotted his presence, all came to talk to him and each one entertained him with cooked chicken and rice and many other foods. He was told that the ancestors of these people had taken refuge there some five centuries before to escape the troublous days of the "First Emperor of China," and that they had remained completely cut off from the rest of human race. They begged the fisherman not to tell anybody about their existence when he left. But the fisherman, though he promised, could not keep this to himself and he marked his route. Then he went to tell the Governor, who immediately dispatched a few men to follow the fisherman. Alas, the marks could not be found. A noted poet of the time heard of this and made an attempt to find this region but in vain. Since then no one has tried.

The fisherman was insincere in his promise, though his inquiring mind was understandable. My New York friend had not been asked not to tell me about the Hidden Forest, nor was I told not to go and find it. However, I felt that I was a little inquisitive, too. If fairies were living there, they would not be interested in seeing me. I hope no one will be influenced by me to find the Hidden Forest on Nantucket.

My return journey to Boston was on the same boat which had brought me to Provincetown. The guide on Nantucket had said that Nantucket had been growing nearer and nearer to Boston since the days when the tea, some of which caused the Boston Tea Party, was carried on Nantucket whaling ships *Dartmouth, Eleanor,* and *Beaver.* Soon the grey-violet dusk was falling over the sea and my mind became intoxicated, rippling along the beat of the waves against the bow of the boat. There were a myriad motions on the sea, yet the waves looked exquisitely restful in their rhythmic movement. The moon had risen to paint a mobile painting with silver-golden lines intricately woven into a forever-moving pattern on the dark blue background of the sea. This mobile painting, though age-old, has not yet been imitated by the ultra-modernist in art. Man cannot paint a mobile painting, though mobile sculpture has now long established itself. The moon was now quite high. Idly watching, idly dreaming thus, I recalled many travels on the sea.

The moon escorted our boat with unfailing care, until I could recognise the silhouetted image of the tower of the Boston Custom House above a massive black heap—Beacon Hill.

Involuntarily, I whispered: "The Atlantic Ocean still belongs to Boston."

Beach along L Street

Sea and sky are one color without horizon.
A lonely seagull repeatedly examines me
Asking suddenly who is more leisurely.
"Well, either you or me," echoed I.

A strong wind, and the seagull can no longer stand.
He has to ride the wind and go
Up and up, floating in the air.
How is it better than my freedom?

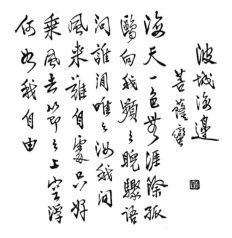

VII

Boston Seasons

T H E R E are many open spaces in other cities like the Common in Boston, but none of them can indicate the time, weather, and seasons as well as Boston Common can. Boston Common is situated in a prominent part of the city and the visitor hardly loses sight of it. During my stay at Pinckney Street on Beacon Hill I crossed Boston Common more than once each day.

I learnt many things about it. It was there that herds of cattle used to be pastured. It was there that John Hancock once ordered his servants to milk every cow found regardless of ownership after he learned that his own cows did not give enough milk. It was there that the same Hancock was arrested, when driving a hackney coach in and out of Boston between the Sunday hours of midnight and sunset without a warrant from a Justice of the Peace. It was there that troops used to drill. It was there that Quakers and witches were hanged. It was there that three hundred young maidens sat at their spinning-wheels and spun to encourage the promotion of industry in America. It was also there that a young girl, a niece of the authoress of *Little Women*, when she wanted to scream, was told to go and do so. But these things are all of the past. Many a girl screamed on Boston Common in my hearing, but I doubt if they were sent there by a famous aunt.

The clock of Boston Common may not have been exact, but it was interesting to me. Between seven-thirty and nine-

thirty in the morning and after five for an hour or so in
the afternoon everyone was dashing to work or from it.
From ten o'clock onwards there would be people strolling
along at a leisurely pace, meditating, amusing themselves

Siesta on Boston Common

by throwing crumbs to the birds, or smoking on the benches
as if they owned the Common. From twelve to two o'clock
the self-employed persons would all disappear, and coming
in their place would be many male shop assistants and office
clerks to sit or lie in all possible poses on the slope in front
of the State House for a nap after lunch. I never saw a woman
in their midst. Someone told me that Boston was essentially
a woman's city, but I disagreed, for I thought Boston Common belonged to men for at least two hours during lunch

time, or even for the whole morning. After two o'clock
Boston Common changed hands. Women took over. Some
might be knitting, some dozed by the side of a perambulator,
some threw a ball to a young boy or girl, and some became
annoyed at the ingratitude of the pigeons who would take
no more crumbs, emptied their bags, and walked away. By
that time all the birds had had more than they could eat
—even the gluttons, pigeons and blackbirds. There would be
more dogs running over the Common then than in the
morning. Nowhere have I seen a greater variety of dogs
than on Boston Common. The different breeds could easily
outnumber the types of human beings. This means that not
many genuine Boston folk appear on the Common. Really,
they are seldom seen there, but before they open their mouth
their manner of walking with their dogs betrays them.

By five o'clock the genuine old Boston folk still observed
the custom of the Puritan days, retired to their homes and
were seen no more for the rest of the day. Boston Common
was then taken over chiefly by young men and women.
Perhaps it would be more exact to say that it was then
owned by young sailors and their girl-friends, for there is
a navy recruiting office and a naval club in the Common
not far from Tremont Street. They were seldom seen to sit
still or stand still. They were to be seen round the naval
club for at least two hours or more after dark. But from
seven till nine o'clock the public benches along the side by
Tremont Street would all be occupied by those who either
had relations in or were connected with the Boston Police
force as well as those who lived in the quarter round the
old North Church where the replicas of Paul Revere's
lanterns are kept. They either talked in the language which
Leonardo da Vinci used or that in which the father of
Eugene O'Neill expressed himself. I saw them playing chess,

shuffling cards and heard them conversing in loud voices as if they were about to stage a fight. They never fought, as far as I remember. Sometimes I saw them in a large group discussing and arguing on current topics as their counterparts would do in Hyde Park, London, on Saturdays and Sundays. They never seemed to slack off on a single Sunday on Boston Common when I was about.

I should say that Boston Common can tell the seasons of Winter and Summer better than those of Spring and Autumn. Winter, when all the trees become leafless and slender, makes Boston Common look emptier and bigger. Every monument and statue reveals itself to visitors. In summer the trees seem to cling together, while in winter they stand apart, silhouetted against the snow-covered ground. Before the coming of snow the city workers are busy laying wooden boards above the footpaths in Boston Public Gardens, which were originally a part of the Common. When the snow had fallen and the Frog-pond was frozen, an unusual noise of happy chatter and laughter could be heard all round, for the youngsters skated almost every afternoon. I have watched them on several occasions—some fell, some quickly picked themselves up again, and some even did square-dancing. The ice on the Frog-pond is undoubtedly thicker than the ice which forms on the pools in Oxford Portmeadow by the Thames River, where I saw skaters fall through the ice often. The Frog-pond remained frozen for days during my stay in Boston.

When summer came to Boston the unusual noise of happy chatter and laughter soon switched over to the swimming pool and the Roman fountain on the Common. The bright blue bottom of the swimming pool often seemed to me to disturb the very pleasant air of Boston Common on purpose, but on hot summer days it was hidden by pink and tanned limbs and faces, dripping with water, so that the air around seemed cooler and refreshing. At the base of the fountain sat many young boys, laughing as the water sprayed over their bodies. Fortunately it was 1953 and not 1802, when the law pursued Sabbath-breakers for bathing at the foot of the Common. I felt glad to know that there were people who could laugh at the law in those dictatorial days, as illustrated by the following verse in the *Centinel* at the time:

> In Superstition's days, 'tis said,
> Hens laid two eggs on *Monday*,
> Because a hen would lose her head
> That laid an egg on Sunday.
>
> Now our wise rulers and the law
> Say none shall wash on Sunday;
> So Boston folks must dirty go,
> And wash them twice on Monday.

While the happy chatter and laughter is going on in the swimming pool and the fountain, something similar, though gentler, is happening on the Frog-pond, particularly when the tulips are in full bloom. That is the coming and going of the Swan boats, with loadfuls of happy faces across the blue sky at the bottom of the pond. Many more happy faces look on. Swans did not pay Boston Public Garden a visit while I was there, so why were the boats swan-shaped? No one could tell me.

The swan boats in Boston Public Garden operate from May until September, I understand. During that period a new event took place in the grounds of the Public Garden. It was the Boston Art Festival. A number of tents sheltered the exhibits of paintings over quite an area, while sculptures stood around, out of doors. Music was relayed through loudspeakers. I made a round of the paintings and found my friend Tseng Hsien-Ch'i's work with pleasant surprise. Tseng's work derives from the ancient Chinese tradition, and the whole show revealed the trend in modern American calligraphic art. Chinese painting derives from Chinese ancient

A Boston castle

scripts which are never realistic but idealistic, imaginative, and suggestive. Chinese calligraphy developed together with Chinese painting, aiming at liberating the visual beauty of graphic movement in lines and color. Modern art of the West and Chinese art are approaching the same goal.

The Art Festival brought many people to the Boston Public Gardens and accentuated the feeling of summer under the bright sunlight. Has Boston a spring season? I missed seeing it in 1953, for I spent February, March, and April in San Francisco that year. When I came back in May, spring was over in Boston, I was told. Spring pays Boston a very brief visit. There is a Spring Street in Boston; I think it is named after water rather than after the season. When spring came, though brief, it touched many parts of Boston.

Its presence in Boston Common was not noticeable except over the flower beds of the Public Garden. But it called on more houses along Commonwealth Avenue than other places, for the magnolias outside them bloomed with hilarious smiles.

I met spring in the Arnold Arboretum on a few occasions. In other words, I went there every two or three days while spring lasted. My Chinese friends at Cambridge did not understand why I had to go there so often, for I am no student of botany. I think one is apt to be mad about something at some time or another in one's life. There should not be any need to explain it. I say this because I do not wish to be psychoanalyzed. I was walking between the trunks of the cherry trees under an umbrella of blossom when suddenly a pheasant gave me a loud scolding and flew away in disgust at my presence. I discussed with a friend the stately manner of the Chinese yulan (*Magnolia denudata* and sometimes called *Magnolia conspicua*) and its clear scent. Two of these yulans stand blooming by the side of the office building. Near them are a few of the white-petalled Japanese species which has a decorative pretty-pretty value only. I also noticed many mountain azaleas and rhododendrons which came originally from west China, particularly from Yunnan Province. This reminded me that the first Director of the Arnold Arboretum, Professor Charles Sprague Sargent, sent Ernest Henry Wilson on several trips to collect plants from China. Through Wilson, many plants in American gardens, public and private, have come from China. Many Chinese plants were given names after Wilson.

David McCord of Wadsworth House, Cambridge, knows all the trees in Harvard Yard and took me to see a small but beautiful beech grove in Brookline and a new road lined with Chinese gingko trees on both sides. When I told

him that I had found a Chinese Scholar Tree in the Boston
Public Gardens, he was surprised, and we discussed how
the word *scholar* came to be used as a qualification for a
tree. I really could not tell, but thought the tree is called
Huai in Chinese and was usually planted near the house
so that it could give shade to scholars at their study.

Besides Spring Street, there is a Summer Street and also
a Winter Street in Boston, although one has to go to West
Roxbury to find an Autumn Street. Autumn does not paint
Boston as brilliantly red and yellow as it does the countryside of all the New England states. Probably it feels it unnecessary, for at the arrival of autumn almost everyone in
Boston either talks of the Indian Summers they have seen
in the past or sets off to see this year's in the country. What
an odd name "Indian summer" is for the season of autumn!
In all Boston newspapers there are articles about the season,
some even describing the route to a fine display of color.
Walter and Jane Whitehill motored me over all the Indian-
summer sightseeing routes from New Hampshire to Vermont,
driving over the Green Mountains from Bennington to
install me at a place at Stowe, through the late Willard
Cogswell's introduction, to enjoy the color up Mount Mans-
field for ten days. Van Wyck and Gladys Brooks took me
along the gold-heaped shores of the Housatonic River in
Connecticut. Phyllis Reaks and her parents drove me round
the red-and-purple-carpeted hills outside West Providence
in Rhode Island. Storer Lunt had me staying with him in
the village inn in Dorset to look at the autumn mountains
in rain, when we were nearly stranded by the floods from
the rivers of Connecticut. I saw the Indian summer of New
England in all its brilliance and in all moods, and it was
unlike any display of color I had seen before. I had not
imagined that there could be such a great variety of oak
trees and that the leaves of the different maples could turn

so brilliantly red against the bright New England sun. It
is the maples and oaks which design the Indian summer for
New England. I was told that the best of the fall colors only
last for at most two weeks.

One afternoon, Donald Messenger, of the *Christian
Science Monitor* at the time, suggested taking me to see
Autumn around Jamaica Pond. I saw enough maples with
red leaves to mingle and intermingle with the masses of
golden and half-golden ones of the elms for a break in the
monotony. There was a mild, pleasant feeling in the air.
We went to have a look in the Children's Museum nearby.
There were all sorts of stuffed animals, birds, and flower
specimens together with dolls in different costumes to keep
children interested.

The next morning I took Shu-li Yang rowing on Jamaica
Pond. There was nobody in the boating office at first, and
we only got a boat after a long wait. Apparently not many
people come to row on the pond. The boats by the shore
were there for anglers to hire. An old woman hesitated to
rent us a boat, for we told her that we had no fishing license,
though she did not bother to see that we had no fishing rods
either. However, I managed to get the boat into the center
of the pond after a struggle, for the boat, squarish in shape,
was constructed only for shifting from one place to another,
not like the rowing boats I got used to on the Thames River
in England. My clumsy handling of the unfamiliar boat
caused Shu-li to laugh at my boast of being an old hand at
rowing. That was an unexpected joke. The sun was bright
but not hot; there were ripples giggling and hurrying on
the water. And the morning air was not chilly either. In fact,
the morning mist had long dispersed and left the autumn
sky as high as it has ever seemed to be. What an azure color
the Boston sky can be at this time of the year! Usually I
saw the leaves on the tree-tops pasted right against the

face of the sky, but now I saw them far apart and far below it; even the tallest elms around the shore became unimaginably low. Our boat was still away from the trees. When we came nearer I saw the leaves flickering like small pieces of gold and brass in and out of the light in tumultuous masses. They were dancing, they were busy, yet so effortlessly. The mild air exhilarated the whole scene. Now we were moving back towards our starting point. Facing us came a troop of a countless quacking army from Duckland, a small island in the center of the pond with two little picturesque willows for decoration. Neither of us raised our hands to wave to them as a sign of welcome, for we had no crumbs to throw, which made Shu-li feel very sad. The leaders of the line cast us a sharp look from their bead-eyes and turned away towards two youngsters standing on the rugged roots of a huge willow tree that stuck into the water. We could not see properly what they were doing there, though Shu-li's eyes are better than mine. I let the boat drift for a moment and was astonished at the continuous line of ducks plunging down into the water from the little island to join the others in a semicircle as if under a strict order. As soon as they were near the willow roots, they broke their line and scattered into a massive cloud of dark-headed tadpoles with heads above the water instead of below. Their movements were swift and their quacking, though deafening, was not altogether disagreeable. Perhaps they were echoing the laughter of the youngsters on the willow-roots or the gentle giggling of young Shu-li in our boat. The mellow air of the pleasant autumnal surroundings had caused them to be so agreeable. The ripples on the water, illuminated by the bright sun, turned the reflection of the autumn leaves of the trees into well-ripened yellow Indian corn coming out of an old Chinese agricultural blowing-machine. The ducks were busy catching it. Or the reflection of the autumn leaves changed the ripples into mysterious jewels, glimmering with dewy flames of amethysts and topazes. The ducks were floating on thin sheets of golden silk, too. All of a sudden came a big "bang" from an automobile a little distance away on the main road. Sudden masses of wings flapped in the air and almost blackened half the sky at first. Many of them flew high above our heads. I bent backwards to look at the flying ducks dotted all over the azure sky. It was a beautiful background for a beautiful pattern, I thought. But my right hand slipped off the handle of the oar. Shu-li quickly gave me the support of her hands with a hearty laugh. The warm colors of yellow, pink, and red breathed warmth all over us. Of all Boston experiences, rowing on Jamaica Pond in the beautiful autumn is one of my most memorable.

Jamaica Pond

On Jamaica Pond
Ducks float in rank and file
Accompanying me to enjoy the autumn light.
Finding no food for them
They turn away.
How frivolous!

Our leaf-like boat
Drifts with the wind at will.

結美亨塘鴨成行

伴我食遊別才太

芎食遊別才太

輕挹一葉舟随風

盈漾

VIII

Boston Eyes

U N L I K E Boston noses, Boston eyes do not require me to find out what they look like but to observe *what* they are looking at. I am still not sure of recognizing a Boston nose. But if I see a pair of eyes always gazing towards the road to Concord, I am positive that their owner is a genuine Boston or Boston-plated man, as Thomas Bailey Aldrich put it about himself.

I had been living in Boston for several months and the place I had been urged and taken to see most frequently was Concord and its vicinity. Almost everyone of the friends I have made in Boston has wanted to show me Concord. The road from Boston to Concord is the most important road in America, they say, a road along which the history of America was created, a road that launched American freedom and a road that marked the beginning of early American literature. I was shown the room which John Hancock and Samuel Adams shared until the night when they were wakened by Paul Revere to flee. I learnt with great interest that the expression, "Put your John Hancock here" means "Sign your name first." John Hancock was the first to sign the Declaration of Independence and his signature was conspicuous and meticulous. I learnt in the old Munroe Tavern that the first President of America dined there, but the tiny little feet of Anna Munroe, the daughter of the first proprietor, caught my imagination more. She was not pretty but had a nice figure and tiny little feet. A young

Swan Boat in Boston Public Garden

Concord Bridge in Indian Summer

minister of the town, named William Muzzy, was courting
her but not sure of his own judgment. So one day he asked
a classmate of his at Harvard College to come and dine
there. Afterwards he sought his friend's opinion of the
proprietor's daughter. The answer was: "Well, I think she
has a devil of a face, but the form and foot of an angel
—and all's well that ends well." It was news to me that
two hundred years ago Harvard students had the same admiration for the tiny feet of girls as Chinese men used to
have. Chinese men admired them for their daintiness and
gracefulness in walking. Unfortunately the Chinese created
a fashion for small feet and indirectly made thousands of
Chinese girls suffer untold pain to have their feet deformed
into an unnaturally small size by being bound when very
young. That custom stopped several decades ago. The Harvard students' admiration did not have such dire effects.

At Concord the first thing to see was the Concord Bridge,
the monument of the Minuteman and then the Old Manse.
There is a monument of the Minuteman in Lexington too.
Artistically speaking, I think the Lexington one, with ir-
regular rocks as its pedestal, has a better setting than its
Concord counterpart.

At first I thought Emerson, being born not too long after
the establishment of American Independence, chose Concord
as his home out of respect for the historical importance of
the place. But the Old Manse told me that his grandfather
was a minister of the local parish church before Concord
changed history. Why did Hawthorne come to live in Concord instead of Salem, to which his wife belonged? Was
it because he did not like Salem much, as he did not enjoy
his work in the Custom House there? He rented the Old
Manse for his honeymoon. Perhaps he wanted to choose a
memorable place for his first month of marriage in the way

that many young married couples of today choose Washington D.C.? The Alcotts perhaps just happened to live in Concord for no particular reason. I feel the characters of Louisa Alcott's *Little Women* are still living somewhere in

The Old Manse at Concord

the Western Hemisphere if there were another Louisa Alcott to describe them. The setting would be different, but the essence could be the same. The chief factor in the difference in setting would be *time*. What interested me was that the area of Concord was not big and the nature of the place not really important, yet it was made so by the unexpected happening of John Hancock's visit to his fiancee while Samuel Adams was in hiding there with a price on his head. Historical events are all accidental, and Concord never had any design to be so important in the History of America, I am sure.

Peking, though not the spot where the history of China

began, has seen much glory and sorrow, too. The glories of
the great Ming dynasty ended in 1644. It was not the fault
of the last Ming ruler, Emperor Ch'ung-Cheng, who was regarded as a well-learned monarch, kind and capable. But on
the 9th of April, Peking fell into the hands of the Manchus.
During the night before the arrival of the invaders, the
Emperor refused to flee; instead he slew the eldest Princess,
ordered the Empress to end her own life before falling into
the enemy's hand, and sent his three sons into hiding. At
the next dawn no one came to the Court Assembly after
the striking of the bell, and the Emperor then descended
from his throne and walked up the Wan-Shou-Shan, a small
hill in the palace grounds, and wrote the following words on
the lapel of his royal robe as his last decree: "I, poor in
virtue and of contemptible character, have incurred the
wrath of the Spirit of Heaven. Being deceived by my ministers, I am ashamed to face my ancestors; I therefore take
off the imperial hat from my head and cover my face with
my hair to await the rebels and invaders to dismember my
unworthy body. But please do not hurt a single one of my
people!" Later the Emperor was found hanged on a tree,
dead. His last words have turned all Chinese eyes towards
Peking, particularly to Wan-Shou-Shan, for the past four
hundred years or so, simply because the Emperor did not
run away from his people and instead took his life to save
the masses from being wantonly slaughtered. He was brave
and acted benevolently. That is why he has been remembered more than many other great emperors in Chinese
history. However, I am inclined to think that remembrance
of him will probably end with my generation. The generation after mine will read history differently. As a matter
of fact, I myself read history nowadays with a different at-
titude towards things from what I used to have. This is

not only because I have grown older but because the events occurring today cannot be compared with those in the past.

It is a common belief that history repeats itself, but I venture to think that history has not repeated itself since the beginning of the history of America. The history of America started with a definite principle of liberty, which was not in existence before. If that principle is still held fast, there cannot be another Concord for the generations after mine to come and see as I was told to do by Boston eyes.

No doubt the Boston eyes of successive generations will still be fixed in the direction of the road to Concord. I cannot and need not speculate as to how people will think of Concord a thousand years hence. Nevertheless, to my mind, Concord has been very fortunate not to have become a Peking, including all the area of Boston as the Capital of America. Otherwise I would not have been able to hear my Boston friends saying, "Concord is as pleasant and peaceful as ever before." Indeed it is so, but it must have been through some changes. For instance, the wooden bridge that arches over the Concord River today is not the one which used to be a public thoroughfare in Paul Revere's days. Perhaps just because it is not a public thoroughfare now, the river there seems to be more peaceful than elsewhere. The monument of the Minuteman hidden behind trees is not easy to see, and is an unassuming one compared to the monuments of war heroes on the European Continent. I have never seen a place of great historic importance so in harmony with its name.

Like Boston eyes, my neither-almond-shaped-nor-quite-slanting pair always turn towards Concord whenever I think of three incidents connected with my presence on the road there or back. The late Ralph Morris took his sister, Dr.

Elizabeth Morris, and me along the heavy-snow-covered road to Concord after Christmas 1953. Ralph had something special in mind to show me. We looked at both the local churches with their typical New England whitewashed walls and spire and tower. They always stand out neat and graceful against the colors of spring, summer, and autumn. I never thought they could be so elegant and serene in the reflection of heavy winter snow. The coming of winter dusk with the subdued white of the snow all along the roadside cast its spell upon my imagination. Despite the constant moving of our car, the shadow of the great change that accompanied the passage of day was as furtive and mysterious as ever. Beyond the area of streetlighting, the road was now very dark. The modern means of lighting up the streets of towns and villages into daylight has its limitation. I was thinking of how quick the stepping-out of day into night was when the car stopped. Ralph Morris led us into a side road where we were suddenly confronted with myriads of small blue lights covering all the branches of three huge elm trees. They looked not quite like elms but like trees of *fire-flowers,* something like fireflies of unusual size stuck on the twigs in millions. My eyes became blind for a minute and were still dazzled by the unusual and fairy-like beauty that closed them. This was what Ralph Morris and his sister had wanted me to see before it vanished. It was the fancy of the local nursery owner to spend a whole month before Christmas fixing more than three thousand blue electric bulbs in the three elm trees. The elms then became unusual Christmas trees and attracted people from far and wide. Each of them went into the nursery, like us, for a look. The wife said to us that it was too much work to put those bulbs in the trees and that her husband would not attempt it again. I thanked the Morrises for having taken me to see this sight, which

Paul Revere on his ride to Concord could never have dreamed of.

Another time at the suggestion of Kuang-Ching Liu, six of us including four of the Yang family and me went to dine at the old Wright Tavern. We were given a room to ourselves. The tavern was very well-kept inside and its fresh atmosphere struck me at once. Neither the manageress nor the waitresses bothered to tell us the history of the inn as their counterparts in Europe had often done on account of my flat face. There must have been plenty to say about Major Pitcairn, who was there on the morning of the 19th of April, 1775. Perhaps the people of the Wright Tavern had no time to spare from catering. Or they took for granted our knowledge of Concord history. I felt gratified that we could concentrate on enjoying the real New England food. The food was good and the service was good and we all talked of our pleasant evening there often afterwards. It was a memorable evening for the youngest member of our party, Te-cheng Yang, then only five. It was his first time to dine out; it was his first time to sit at a big dining table with grown-ups and it was his first time to eat a three-course American dinner. We were all feeling a bit uneasy about his table manners before we sat down. But he charmed the waitresses at once. One of them whispered to me: "He behaves like a grown-up. What a perfect young *gentleman* he is!" Both Lien-sheng and Miu-chen, his parents, were pleased with the remark, but it interested me in another way. I had not heard a similar remark before, and I think perhaps it could be heard only in New England where the air of old England has not vanished without a trace. Besides, in most of the restaurants in the United States they keep young good-looking girls, who take orders with a sort of *uniform* smile, without any real interest in what they are doing.

The third time was on the Concord River. Tseng Hsien-Ch'i, of the Asiatic Department of the Boston Museum of Fine Art, wanted to take me out for a drive. I jokingly said that I would like to go boating for a change, for during my many years in Oxford, England, I used to row on the Isis, the Cherwell, and the Thames, though punting is still beyond my skill. Hsien-Ch'i signalled me to get in the car and drove on without a word. A splendid companion for silent travelling he was at that moment. I thought some landmarks looked familiar and was not surprised when Hsien-Ch'i remarked that we were on the road to Concord. The signs of autumn hung all along the way. There were wooden structures piled with bright orange pumpkins, purple and red apples, spotted corn with protecting leaves, and many other shiny green vegetables in front of a shop or on the roadside. Sometimes the fruit and vegetables were just scattered on the doorsteps or by the footpath. They made lovely splashes of color. I asked Hsien-Ch'i to let me out at a number of places and made a few sketches of the displays. He agreed that they were highly paintable. This kind of New England country store springs up like mushrooms all over the New England states from September onward. Concord Country Store was the first to make its appearance, a number of years ago, and was so successful that all the others followed. How colorful the road to Concord has become!

When he had parked the car, Hsien-Ch'i asked someone where we could get onto the river. After going a short distance through a wood and over a newly-built stone bridge, we found a landing stage with three canoes lying airing, bottoms upwards, on the shore. No rowing boat was in sight and no one had ever heard of a *punt*. At first I declined to get into a canoe, for I had had an experience of being overturned in a rubber canoe in the Isis in Oxford. "The English canoe is round-bottomed, but the American one is flat," Hsien-Ch'i said with an expert air. A small boy ran away from his playmates along the riverside and came to look at us gleefully. He grinned broadly at my not wanting to go into a canoe. I noticed that he had no front teeth which made him look more mischievous. Suddenly I remembered the great Chinese wit, Chang Hsuan-tzu, of Han dynasty about the second century B.C. When he was only eight years old and had lost several teeth, someone laughed at him and said: "What are you going to do with those dog-holes in your mouth?" "They are there," answered young Chang, "to let puppies like you run in and out." I kept my mouth shut, for young American boys might be sharper than Chang.

A push by the owner of the canoe sent us to the middle of the stream. I soon found the flat-bottomed canoe stable and comfortable. We paddled on, one after the other, as if we were the two "Fur traders descending the Missouri" painted by George Caleb Bingham in about 1845, or like the canoeing figures in some of Winslow Homer's water-color sketches. But Homer loved stormy waves and foaming rocks. And the Missouri is wide. We were just slowly skimming along the Concord. It was pleasant and agreeable. Reeds and willows bordered most parts of the stream. I could see the roots of many water-plants dangling underneath us, swaying with the current, though the surface we moved on was completely unruffled except by our paddles. The water seemed to be immeasurably deep, for it was an unusually dark green. Here and there I noticed masses of translucent yellow and red dots. They were the reflection of the leaves of the trees lining one side. Behind them showed the white-and-yellow-washed walls of a house or two. Some small figures in bright scarlet and blue sweater and shorts moved in and out, as if playing hide-and-seek. Our canoe was the only one to be seen. Yet no one came to the shore for a look at us. So we paddled on.

Taking to flight

The bright sun still shone brightly; the stillness of the air became more intense, and the easy motion of the canoe under each stroke of the paddles was audible. The charm of autumnal Nature along the Concord River was ethereal and affecting—impossible to express in words. Unexpectedly a gentle breeze rustled through the long reeds close by our canoe and created a hissing sound. Following the sound, there flew out several colored dragonflies, one of which was royal blue, making a striking spot in the air. They darted forward at a good pace, stood still for a moment, and darted off again. Far in the distance flapped a large grey heron, which became smaller and smaller until it was lost to sight. Where did the heron come from? Had it caught a fish in its beak? And where had it stood before? I was paddling in front and had the advantage of seeing the view without obstruction. That was Hsien-Ch'i's idea. He is a very understanding friend and did not urge me to paddle harder. As a matter of fact, our canoe drifted most of the while, and backwards too. We took our time.

I have a passion for watching a heron standing motionlessly and patiently near a river shore or lake shore. But the heron is a very shy bird. The slightest stir in the air can send it flapping away. I have never got very close to one of them. On the other hand, the flight of a heron skimming over a long river affords me endless joy: it is a subject which I love to portray.

A stone bridge now came in sight. It was still a good distance away. By and by we heard splashing of water as well as chattering and laughter near the shore beyond a group of long reeds. A few young boys were swimming there. Perhaps they had caused the flight of the heron. They made me chuckle, for I remembered the following old Chinese joke:

A doctor had mismanaged a seriously ill patient whose family seized and detained him for the night in order to bring him to the law. After midnight he managed to free himself and escaped by swimming across a river. When he got home, he found his son still studying medicine hard. He sighed and said to the son: "You need not read too much in books; the first and most important thing is to learn to swim."

At that moment one of the boys was pushed into the water and caused a great splash. The rest laughed louder than before. Hsien-Ch'i thought I was laughing with the boys, so he joined the chorus before we entered the arch of the bridge. We had now come to a part of the river which remains as rustic as it can have been even before the days of the early Northern American Indians. A large patch of muddy marsh piled with dead leaves and newly-fallen ones stretched out into the river and made our canoe swerve.

The sun had gone down, and we turned to the west as if we were trying to follow. The river became a shining strip of mirror glass which reflected the sky, bare of clouds. There seemed to be a huge sheet of indigo blue spread over the bottom of the river, with the reflected autumnal leaves and twigs of the trees and bushes for the frieze. I did not want to dip my paddle but we had to. Each dip of the paddles caused a magic vibration of the mirror glass. When we paused and the mirror glass resumed its flat surface I saw that the bottom of the river was no longer pure blue in color. There were a number of white strips of cloud and there was bright light to light them up, with golden lines round their edges. When I lifted up my head, we were now facing a wooden bridge—the famous Concord Bridge—guarded by a number of irregular trees whose leaves flickered and danced in the light of the bright sunset as if they were made of sparkling gold or red-hot brass. The sky was completely drunk. Now the strips of white clouds turned a translucent red and pink. They helped to bring the whole scene into communion with our eyes. Fortunately the darkish grey color of the wooden bridge calmed the exhilaration of the view and revealed its crowning secret as the delicate loveliness of autumnal Nature. Nowhere had I met a more satisfactory composition for a painting and I made a sketch. I felt glad that the history of America did begin at Concord bridge and that no future Americans would try to build a steel bridge over the Concord River at this point. The bridge here will remain in wood for a long time to come and the lovely autumnal scene will repeat itself year after year.

We did not go under Concord bridge but followed the same way back to where we had started, content and in leisurely manner. I thanked Hsien-Ch'i for the outing, and though all Boston eyes may turn towards Concord for American history as well as for early American literary association, mine will always turn to look for the autumnal scene at Concord bridge.

Concord Bridge

Autumn colors saturate
My eyes with blazing light.
Idly we talked of the night when Revere
    sped reporting on flying horse;
The Minutemen by upholding arms in a single
    battle established a country.
Long live Concord Bridge!

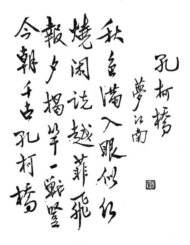

IX

Boston Ears

N E W Y O R K has many "tallests," "biggests," and "largests,"
but Boston has more "firsts." I found the First Baptist
Church, First National Bank, First Stone Church in Boston,
First United Presbyterian Church, the First Christian Science Church. I was told that Boston was the first city to set
aside a piece of ground for a Common, by laying out Boston
Common in 1634; Boston opened the first public school in
1635, published the first newspaper in 1690, started the first
revolution with bloodshed in 1770, built the first railway in
1825, was the location of the first ether operation in 1846,
made the world's first telephone call in 1876, and created
the first subway in 1895. None of these "firsts" interests me
more than the first use of Boston ears.

Of course Boston cocked her ears to the various pulpits,
to the different orations and proclamations during the
Colonial days and the Revolutionary period. But Boston ears
met an unprecedented check through the "Act to Prevent
Stage Plays and other Theatrical entertainments" in 1750.
So Boston ears must by then already have been put to good
use in the world of public amusement. The act was passed
when Boston was under the strict rule of the Puritans. No
hackney coach was then allowed to drive in and out between
the Sunday hours of midnight and sunset without a warrant
from a Justice of the Peace. None of the vehicles in the town
was then permitted to move faster than the movement of
a pedestrian on the road when the church service was on.

I thought how peaceful Boston Sundays must have been and how enjoyable it would have been to do some silent-travelling there then, though I would no doubt have encountered trouble on my way.

It is said that many progressive-minded men of Boston tried to repeal the Act to Prevent Stage Plays and other Theatrical entertainments, but without avail. So they used their minds in another progressive way. The ears of Boston lovers of the drama erected a stage and gave it the name, "New Exhibition Room," in Board Alley, which is now Hawley Street. They advertised their plays as "moral lectures" with demonstrations of actual vice or virtue. *"Venice Preserved"* by Otway was advertised as one lecture in five parts to exemplify the dreadful effects of conspiracy. Shakespeare's *Macbeth* was promoted as "A Dialogue on the Horrid Crime of Murder, by Mr. and Mrs. Smith." Suchlike lectures went on for a good while. Though my own head condition might be described by some modern doctors as "cerebral atrophy," I am always full of admiration for the resourcefulness of our human brain. No matter how minute the laws and regulations devised by some brains are, there are always other brains to find a way to evade them.

Though John Hancock himself suffered arrest for hackneying on the Lord's Day, he actually caused the arrest of one of the actors, named Harper, when the play, *The School for Scandal,* was performed on a night of December in 1792 in that New Exhibition Room. The performance came to a sudden end, but the audience did not allow the house to be closed before a group of young men pulled down the portrait of Governor Hancock and trampled it under their feet as a protest. It is gratifying to note that in those strict Puritanical days of Boston people were much better off than those living under a totalitarian ruler of today, for they

could trample their ruler's portrait under their feet to show
their disapproval. Eventually, in 1794, the first true theater
was built by Bullfinch from a classic design, on Federal
Street. I have read that the effect of Sabbath Observance
lasted until the beginning of 1800, when the theater, now
established, omitted Saturday night performances. There
were still just five evening performances a week even after
the best-known old Boston Theater was opened in 1852.
The plays played there were chiefly Shakespeare's, and many
noted actors and actresses played there before theater land
developed in New York. The Boston audience gained such
a reputation for its ears and eyes that New York theater
managers have always liked to try their new shows in Boston
first, just as London theater managers like to try theirs in
Oxford.

To my great satisfaction and happiness I learnt that the
first comedy, called "The Contrast," ever written by a native
American was by Royall Tyler, great-grandfather of my
friend, William Royall Tyler of the American Embassy in
Bonn, Germany. The play was produced in Boston in 1796
and was a success. The first Royall Tyler, I was told, held
the post of Chief Justice of the Supreme Court of Vermont
from 1807 to 1813.

Boston ears have been exercised to their greatest advantage
in Boston concert halls, particularly the Boston Symphony
Hall.

I am no student of music, though I attended concerts
many a time during my residence in England. But, without
Boston ears, I had better not try to describe what I first
heard of Boston Pops. Nevertheless, it was my first connection with Boston ears as well as my first happy evening
in the Boston musical world. When in New York for the
first time in 1946 I paid several visits to our most prominent

scholar, Dr. Hu Shih, who was living there after having relinquished his post as Chinese Ambassador in Washington, D.C. I went to say farewell to him before my return to England, and met Arthur Walworth, who suggested that I should see Boston. My answer was that that was in my program, for I wanted to see Mr. Kojiro Tomita, Curator of the Asiatic Department of the Boston Museum of Fine Arts and also Dr. Huang Ming-lung, a German-educated Chinese pharmacist, who had been invited to the medical school in Cambridge. The next morning there came to my hotel by *special delivery* a list of the Sixty-first Season of Boston Pops Orchestra with the invitation: "Mr. Chiang, would you like to go to one of these?" I felt grateful. I had only one day for Boston—Thursday, May 2, 1946. After a good tour of the Asiatic Department with Mr. Tomita, I was met by Arthur Walworth at the entrance and was driven to make a quick call at each of the important Boston landmarks before entering Symphony Hall. The inside of the hall was unlike any other music hall, for the seats were not arranged in rows, but were in groups round a table. The audience would sit round the tables drinking and eating while listening to the music. We reached our seats almost as the same time as everybody else. It seemed to me that there were few early or late arrivals, perhaps because Boston is small compared to London, Paris, or New York, and because most of the audience came in their own cars. I always think it is an absolute obligation to show self-respect and re-spect for the conductors, musicians, and players by arriving at a theater or concert hall in good time for the performance. Should one arrive late for one reason or another, one should maintain one's self-respect by forfeiting the pleasure of that evening.

It was a warm May evening. This may have caused the

lack of formal dress in the audience as a whole. Not many women wore evening dress, though quite a few men wore tuxedoes. The Conductor, Arthur Fiedler, bowed to the audience and then turned to start the performance. The audience applauded enthusiastically but not for very long. The programme, which I have kept, was as follows:

Entrance of the Guests into the Wartburg
    from "Tannhauser" (a Pops record) .... Wagner
Gavotte and Finale from the
    "Classical" Symphony .... Prokofieff
Nocturne .... Barbara Curry
Slavonic Dance in G Minor .... Dvořák
"Bostonia" Suite .... Keith Brown
Warsaw Concerto (a Pops record) .... Addinsell
            Piano Soloist: Leo Litwin
Bolero (a Pops record) .... Ravel
Selection from "Carousel" .... Rodgers
Promenade .... Anderson
"Bahn Frei" ("Clear Track") Polka (a Pops record) .... Strauss

There were two short intermissions. During the performance the music seemed to permeate every corner of the hall with dedicated notes and vibrations, without being disturbed by any movement of a single head. The members of the audience sat in a trance, making full use of their Boston ears. After each item there was not much applause, if I remember correctly, but each member of the audience turned to his or her neighbour and their eyes met in a gentle smile as if they were in complete approval of what they had just heard. Before each intermission there was a good round of applause and still more at the end of the programme. On that occasion Boston ears gave me the first fine impression of how well they functioned. It was noteworthy that neither cough nor sneeze disturbed my un-Boston ears throughout the whole evening. Probably this was due to the warmth of May, for I now know that the people of Boston are not immune to coughs and sneezes.

Having thus introduced me to Symphony Hall, Arthur

Square dance

wanted to show me the folk-dancing which was in great vogue at the time. It was rather late at night and everywhere outside was dark when we were at a distance from a street light. We entered a door which seemed to lead to a basement and soon found ourselves standing inside a quite spacious hall, the ceiling of which suggested a barn. Many people were already there. Some wore blue jeans with checked shirts. Neither of us joined in the dance. It was the so-called Square Dance, said to be derived from the dancing of the American Indians. There were two girl dancers wearing long bright scarlet skirts. They made quick, swift movement of their bodies and their skirts flashed startlingly and most attractively, almost making me forget the existence of the dancers themselves. The scarlet skirts reminded me much of Ireland, where the scarlet skirts have long been part of the traditional costume. Presently I was told that the original "Square dance" had developed into a type of Spanish Gypsy dance. My knowledge about dancing is nil; when I asked about the real folk-dance of Boston, it proved to be a very silly question. Nevertheless, I enjoyed the evening, with its unforgettable impression of Boston ears, and I thanked Arthur Walworth wholeheartedly.

Some of my compatriots, who have been working and living round Boston, have developed Boston ears. Dr. and Mrs. Chao Kuo-chun are two of them. The wife, a doctor of biochemistry, works in the Agricultural department of Harvard, and the husband, a doctor of sociology, has been a Research Fellow in Chinese economic and political studies, in Harvard too. Both have found time to go to Concerts and "Pops" now and then, though Kuo-chun once wrote to me that "the aesthetic senses are increasingly dulled by so-called 'social scientific research.' How little time one has nowadays to enjoy the 'things of beauty' for sheer pleasure without utilitarian motifs!" He was urging me to join them for a concert at Tanglewood at which Isaac Stern was playing Beethoven's Violin Concerto. I learned more from Kuo-chun about the Boston "Pops." He said that there was doubt as to the origin of the word, *Pops*. It could be an abbreviation of the word "popular" or could have been inspired by the sound of popping corks which sometimes unintentionally punctuates a *pianissimo* passage. It had already been used by W. S. Gilbert in *Patience*.

> Conceive me if you can—
> An everyday young man,
>   A commonplace type
>   With a stick and a pipe
> And a half-bred black and tan—
>
> Who thinks suburban hops
> More fun than Monday Pops;
>   Who's fond of his dinner,
>   And doesn't get thinner
> On bottled beer and chops.

The Boston Pops were the result of the experiment tried by the four-year-old Boston Symphony Orchestra in 1885 of giving a series of light summer concerts at the end of their winter season. The idea was that the music-lovers could sit around tables drinking and eating food served by aproned waiters in Symphony Hall, while the music played. This sounds like the custom in the theaters in Peking and Shanghai, but my experience inside the Symphony Hall was that the audience almost forgot to drink and eat while the music was played. They really made proper use of their ears. Kuo-chun also gave me a number of names of well-known conductors before Arthur Fiedler took over the direction in 1930.

Arthur Fiedler was the first native Bostonian to assume the baton for the Boston Pops, and it has not changed hands since. Bostonians must be proud of him. To me he is an *exceptional* Bostonian in that neither his father nor his grandfather was born there, nor has he an ancestor in Mount Auburn.

Mr. Chou Wen-chung, the thirty-four-year-old Chinese

composer and winner of the 1957 Guggenheim Memorial Award for Scholars and Artists, was trained at the New England Conservatory of Music. He came to the United States from China about the same time in 1946 as I came from England to New York for the first time. In his years in Boston, he says that he has never missed one single winter season of the Boston Symphony Orchestra and was always in Symphony Hall for the Boston Pops. Among his compositions, Mr. Chou's *Landscapes* was premiered by Leopold Stokowski and the San Francisco Symphony Orchestra in November 1953, and *The Fallen Petals* by the Louisville Orchestra in February 1955. His *Two Miniatures From T'ang* was written in 1957 at the request of Sarah Lawrence College. His Chinese ears, having been trained to be like Boston ears, are now international and have helped him both to make an interesting study of the history of Chinese music and to suggest a fusion of Occidental and Oriental music which, as he puts it, would go far to remove cultural barriers in this new space age of ours. He has found the philosophy and theory of Chinese music well in accord with the spirit of today's tendencies and experiments in music. He has also found the basic musical concept of the two eminent contemporary composers, Anton Webern and Edgar Varese, astonishingly close to that of Chinese musicians. In his study of the history of Chinese music, which dates back some 2,500 years, Mr. Chou says there are many similar musical innovations. For example, the principle of the "cycle of fifths" was discovered by Kuan Tzu in the seventh century B.C., one century before the invention of the Pythagorean scale. These parallels interest me for I always enjoy making comparative studies of things from their beginning and trying to understand why they have developed much better in one place than the other. I tried to learn to play the seven-string lute, Ch'i-hsien-Ch'in in Chinese, in my college days but my defective left ear was a hindrance. Therefore I have no first-hand knowledge of Chinese music, yet my appreciation of it has not diminished. Though the origin of Chinese music dates back to so remote a time, it has not had a similar, or say parallel, development to western music. China never had a state religion, which I consider one factor militating against the development of Chinese music throughout the centuries. Another factor, I think, was the rigidity of Chinese Confucianism since the Han Dynasty (206 B.C.–A.D. 219), which restricted the display of human emotion in public. This was no fault of Confucius, for he himself was very much interested in the early folk songs and collected many of them, including the frankest love songs, into a book of songs, *Shih Ching* in Chinese, one of the Chinese Classics for everybody's study. From the beginning of the present century there came a definite change in the way of Chinese life, for Confucianism relaxed its rigidity over the *moral* relation between man and woman in the face of the invasion of Western civilisation into China. Quite a number of young Chinese who have been trained in Western music have proved themselves good singers of Western songs, or have become violinists or pianists and have appeared on Western platforms from time to time. Now we have Western-trained composers, and Mr. Chou Wen-chung is one of the most noted.

During my stay in Boston I often slipped down Pinckney Street from Beacon Hill to have a stroll on the Storrow Memorial Embankment along the Charles River whenever there was a bright moon above. More than once I found myself sitting on a bench or on the grass to listen to what was being played in the Hatch Memorial Shell. At first I had been surprised to find so many people about and used to hasten my steps to get away from the crowd. However the crowd was there with one united purpose, to listen to good music. When the music was played in the Hatch Shell, few talked or moved. Besides, the ground is spacious and extensive. There is always space between the small groups of people, who as a rule sit on the grass. Even if they whisper or discuss a little, it does not disturb. I was always a group by myself and seldom sat very near the Shell nor other people. I may have kept my Chinese habit from my younger days at home in Kiukiang. Whenever we had artist friends of my father's, an artist himself, or some relation who came to stay and wanted to play the *ti-tzu* or *hsiao,* (Chinese flutes) or Ch'i-hsien-Ch'in, father would always have them play in our garden or in the bamboo grove not far from our home and we would all scatter away from the musician and sit by the shore of a small pond or on the rugged root of a willow tree. It is the Chinese tradition to have music played inside a pine grove or bamboo grove, as can be seen in famous Chinese paintings by Sung masters. We think the notes of the music coming through the pine needles or bamboo leaves become purer and clearer and have a more soothing effect on the ears and the mind. So I sat by myself. Sometimes the gentle breeze came over the Charles River and carried the clear melodies of Bach, Mozart, or Chopin to my un-Boston ears with dreamlike effect in the dream-world of moonlight. Life, though complex in our modern days, can have its moments of being extremely simple.

Arthur Fiedler created these outdoor concerts. He conducted the first in 1929. Then the Hatch Memorial Shell was built, and a big piece of open ground was reserved along the east shore of the Charles River, so that the concerts could become a feature of Boston life. Band-playing in the park is another matter. I have listened to the open-air concerts in San Francisco's Golden Gate Park and also in Chicago, but the atmosphere there was unlike that which I enjoyed in Boston. Arthur Fiedler has the reputation of being equally expert in a performance of a classic or of an up-to-date popular hit, with the correct tradition for the one, and the American bounce and rhythm for the other. My ears, if un-Boston, do not doubt it.

Only once did I find the open ground around the Hatch Shell filled to capacity. It was a very warm July evening in

"I don't know what it's all about."

1953. I went to the riverside for a gentle breeze. As usual, I came to the open ground, which to my amazement was packed with people sitting, standing, applauding and joking. Speeches came through the loudspeakers one after another. As I did not know what it was all about, I did not pay much attention to the speeches. Yet I found it very difficult to make my way through the crowds. I even met more ducks than usual. They were wide awake and quacked in chorus with the applause. Had it not been for their quacking I could easily have tripped over them in the dark. By and by the speeches ended and music began. I eventually got through the people and arrived at the newly built bridge over the road nearby. The bridge was decked with a festoon of coloured lights and thick with people. I stood behind two youngsters who were much shorter than I, facing the Hatch

Shell in the distance. I felt that we were standing on a balcony as if in the company of some Royal personage to wave to the throng underneath. But none of us waved. We were all listening to the music attentively. I tried to remember the scene in order to work out a picture for it. Afterwards I went back to bed pleasantly cool; I still had no idea what had been happening that evening.

In the newspaper I read: Between 30,000 and 35,000 listeners gathered last night to witness the opening ceremonies of the twenty-fifth-year anniversary of the popular outdoor musical programs. Arthur Fiedler, who founded the concerts and has continued as their conductor, was signally honored when Governor Christian A. Herter dedicated a handsome new pedestrian bridge to him, christening it the "Arthur Fiedler Bridge." After receiving a silver baton from Mr. Frank N. Folsom, president of the RCA-Victor Recording Corporation, Conductor Fiedler opened with the "Entrance of the Guests into the Wartburg" from Wagner's *Tannhaüser* and continued with Handel's Water Music Suite, Strauss's Overture to *Die Fledermaus,* Ravel's "Bolero," Leroy Anderson's arrangement of some waltzes by Richard Rodgers, Handel's "Largo" from *Xerxes* (for which Leo Panasevich played a silken violin solo), Tchaikovsky's "Waltz of the Flowers," and a new march by Peter Bodge, "The Governor Herter March."

I folded the paper with a wry chuckle. The ducks and I had been equally unaware of the importance of that occasion for Boston ears.

X

Boston Stone

DAVID McCORD is always busy in the daytime with his duties as the Secretary of the Harvard Fund Council. He also lectures all over the United States. His work as poet and author is therefore done at night. He has twenty books to his credit. He has little time for sleep, nor has he much time to entertain his large number of friends and introduce them to his beloved Harvard and Boston. Yet he loves company and his friends dearly. I shall always think of him clinking glasses and reciting fascinating lines. As well as everything else he is an artist. He has developed an interesting technique of his own. Some of his small sketches show spontaneous cohesion between mind and hand. I like them. The little sketch of a boat with hills behind, which he presented to the poet, Robert Frost, has depth and distance in its few quick lines and touch of wash put on by his finger.

One afternoon David rang me up to ask me to come and see something of special interest to Boston. How he could find time to do it I could not guess. We went to the Widener Library and looked at the diorama models of early three-hilled Boston and the hackney-coach days of Harvard. Then he spoke of the Boston Stone. That was what he wanted to show me. I had just visited Plymouth Rock, which is dated 1620, but had not heard of the Boston Stone. When I said so, David replied that until his series of Broadcasts "About Boston" through Station WBZ, Boston, probably not a dozen people had ever seen the Boston Stone or known of its existence. He told me that it bears the date 1737 and took its name from the London Stone; that it was brought over from England in 1700, originally used as a paint mill by the painter who then occupied the Marshall Street premises, and that it appears later to have been considered as a starting

Boston Stone

point for surveyors and as a direction marker for the local shops. The "Boston Stone" was clearly his pet. He drove me to Marshall Street to see it, but Marshall Street did not anticipate him as a visitor, and had made no provision of parking space for his largish car. We had to walk some distance. The street was quiet in the late afternoon. There was not enough street lighting for us to decipher the words on the stone. I decided to come back in daylight.

David also wanted to show me the everlasting gas torches at Charlestown and the lights of Boston from a height near Bunker Hill. There was still some twilight on Charlestown Bridge as we passed over it. David drove slowly to let me see

the reflection of the intricate steel-structure in the water and
the twinkling stars cast on the water by the electric lights
from the bridge. It was a picture of unusual patterns, light
and colour for fascinating composition. David wished he
could paint it. I marvelled at his artistic taste and conception.
To me Bunker Hill was just the looming dark trunk of a
huge tree with its branches hidden inside the evening sky at
that moment. I did not want to get near it for a close look.
David was at pains to point out a number of old houses built
in the eighteenth century close to the hill. In the faint light
I got little impression of them. He had a great deal to tell
about Wapping Street. It was a narrow, quaint, irregular, and
shabby street, he said, famous for its interesting shop signs,
such as "Everything from a needle to an anchor," or "Don't
risk your money; buy a leg-belt" (where sailors can keep their
money), or "Why get wet when a raincoat is only $1.25?"
All this interested me, and I peered into the dark. Finally
I managed to read a sign, "Eggs sold here, fresh all round."
A story came into my mind, which Professor Arthur Jeffery
of Columbia University is very fond of telling. When he
was finishing his year of study in Edinburgh University,
Scotland, a well-known organist of the time delivered a lecture on organ-playing. Being famous and rather pompous in
displaying his knowledge, he derided those who could not
play any musical instrument, but liked to be critical of the
efforts of those who could. After the lecture, the Rector of
the University remarked gently that he had never laid an
egg but he thought he could tell a good one from a bad one.

Eventually we were standing on open ground, high up
near a hospital. Here there was sufficient light in the sky for
us to see something. We had a fine view of the Charlestown
Bridge with the Boston Custom House and the rest in the
soft evening mist. Unfortunately I had brought nothing with

me with which even to make a rough sketch. On our way
back we had a look at the huge torchlike gaslight fluttering
in the dark grey sky above the pitch-black mass of the gas-
works underneath, like an illustration of a philosophy of
life. Human life has always been something of a black mass
under a dark grey sky, but there has always been some guid-
ing light, too. Has man not been led by some light from the
most primitive type of life to the sputnik age of today?
Regarding sputnik ways, life is still a black mass. But there
is still light to lead us through. I don't see the black too
black. The center of learning is the center of light. As long
as the center of light keeps on burning, there can never be
complete darkness in the world. Sputnik has no light in itself
and cannot destroy a world with so many centers of light.
Cambridge is an important one in the United States and
Boston is another.

When I did visit the Boston Stone in daylight I did not
find out much more than David had told me. The description was engraved on an oblong piece of stone inserted in
the wall of a small antique house in a state of disrepair. The
Boston Stone was underneath the description close by the
doorstep of the house. It could easily be overlooked. I could
not be sure whether the house had any occupants or not. At
the turn into narrow Marshall Street, two old houses joined
together stand near the Boston Stone. One has a wooden shop-
sign "Learnard's: Boston's Oldest Shoe Store, Est. 1800."
There were all kinds of shoes lying on the shelf by the window, but no one inside and no sign of any new shoes being
made there. The door was closed. The other house was not
open either but had a long description in golden letters on
a long wooden board as follows:

1660 Original Building.
Owned and occupied in 1660 by William Courser, Town Crier

and Innkeeper, he being the first Town Crier of Boston.

In 1737 by James Davenport, Brother-in-law of Benjamin Franklin.

Owned from 1764 by Gen. John Hancock, First signer of the
Declaration of Independence.

The Continental Troops were paid here in 1779 by Deputy General Paymaster Ebenezer Hancock.

Boston's Oldest Shoe Store has been located in this building since
1796.

The oldest shoe store

A conviction that these two houses would disappear in
times to come crept into my mind. I have had no such conviction in front of any old building, big or small, in England or
France. There the neighbourhood of any old historic building may change, but it will not change drastically. In America changes are rapid and drastic. Boston with her roots in

American history may be different in this respect. On the other hand, these three houses have nothing to make them memorable, nor any Charles Dickens to bring them fame. There is an old Chinese saying; "Jen Chieh Ti Ling; Ti Ling Jen Chieh" or "Great man makes the place live; important place makes man great."

I thought I had come to Marshall Street early enough to meet few people. But the commotion and noise in the neighbourhood were indescribable. Though I always prefer to travel or stroll silently, I do not mind placing myself in a melting pot so long as I do not get boiled. After my daylight look at the Boston Stone and the oldest shoe store, I came into the midst of shoppers and gazers moving slowly between the pushcarts and vendor-stands lining both sides of North Street. The Boston Saturday Market was in full swing. The day was bright; the sun was not as hot as it can be in the beginning of June; but the loud shouts—"Hey, mister, oranges, bananas, plums, melons, celery, onion . . ."—made me perspire. Horses were standing by their carts; one tossed its head up and down incessantly to get food from its nose-bag, another whinnied intermittently as if calling for attention or for more food, the third kept stamping its right fore-foot on the ground, seeming to tell me off: "Go away, you busybody." A little innocent donkey cast its innocent eye on me and went on eating an endless supply of carrots from the hands of three youngsters, whose mother or mothers were shouting in turn with other vendors close by. I took the horse's hint and found my way out of the market without much delay. The air in an empty street cooled me and I felt happy not to have been boiled. I reflected that the market was not much different from those I had seen in New York, London, Paris, Shanghai, or Peking, or anywhere else. After all, human beings are not really different from one another.

Soon I found myself in another crowded scene—the Quincy Market. There was more room here to move but the smell of fish chased me wherever I went, while the red blood of meat had every opportunity to stain my clothes. So I hurried on towards Adams Square. All around the lower part of Faneuil Hall I noticed the offices of meat wholesalers. I did not linger but entered the Hall for a look. It was built for a market, as a gift from Peter Faneuil in 1742, with a hall for town use above it, in which meetings so important for the future independence of America were held that it became known as "The Cradle of Liberty." The grand, spacious hall on the second floor dates from an enlargement of the building by the famous architect, Charles Bulfinch, in 1805.

On emerging, I stood in Adams Square far from the Adams statue facing Faneuil Hall to gaze up at the top of the weather-vane on the tower of the hall. I knew that the grass-hopper said to have been borrowed by Peter Faneuil from the Royal Exchange of London was still on it, but it was too high up for me to distinguish. Suddenly I chuckled, for the Hall as a whole had revealed itself to me as an enormous woman selling vegetables in the Halles Centrales in Paris. The little round-domed tower was the head, the third and second floors the huge body, with the sun blinds all round as the short, stiff-starched but already dirty apron. My next surprise was the sight of a huge-chested man on my way to have lunch at Durgin Park's. He reminded me of one whom I met in Lowell Street in front of an antique shop when I was strolling along from North Station. Three young children, two boys and one girl, all over ten years of age, stood against his chest and there seemed to be room for two more. An elderly man leaning against a wall not far from the group had looked unimaginably feeble and small. All the shops

Outdoor Concert at night

Copley Square in storm

along Lowell Street are antique shops, chiefly selling glass and china of Dresden and Chelsea type, but also some bronzes and old-type lanterns. An Elevated structure occupies the center of the street, shutting out much light from the shops on both sides.

After lunch I made my way to see the Boston Custom House, which was not far away. It was not easy to see, however, for the streets are narrow and the houses close by not very low. I had no wish to climb up to the top of the inside. The sun had run deep into the clouds. It was much greyer all round than the colour of the stone wall of the Custom House. So I left for the Old State House. While I was moving slowly around it, a middle-aged man standing by me remarked that that little building ought not to have been left there. It looked so odd among all the tall buildings close to it. Another tall building like the Post Office in Milk Street could have been built there. "Just think how many offices it would hold and how much that piece of land would be worth!" I looked at him with a smile and he went away. He had a slight foreign accent. He looked like a naturalised-American banker. His father might have come to live in Boston before him, but not his grandfather. He could have been neither Bostonian nor New Englander. He could not have read America's history book well enough before taking the oath on being naturalised. But he might have argued that there is a good Bulfinch-designed New State House on Beacon Hill, so why keep the Old?

It is true that the Old State House wears a look unlike any of its neighbours. On each side of its roof there is a line of dormers and on the center of the roof stands a squarish tower with a little belfry reminiscent of a Dutch church. In fact, the whole building breathes a Dutch flavour. Its minute size in comparison with the rest of its neighbours groans that it will be squashed into nothing. Yet it has stood its ground since 1713, though it suffered a disastrous fire once. I read somewhere that after the New State House had been finished and had come into use, many voices roared more loudly than

"Will History be sold for money?"

the one I had heard a moment ago that this old building should be destroyed and its site developed. A large sum of money was offered for the development of the site. The voices went on and on for a long while before a decision could be made. Finally the prosperous city of Chicago sent over a message that she would like to buy the whole structure and remove it to the shore of Lake Michigan, brick by brick, in order to show respect to such a great American monument. Immediately this offer spurred Bostonians and New Englanders not to be outdone. So the Old State House was kept for me to see on its original spot.

No doubt I would have been able to see it on the shores of Lake Michigan. Somehow I would not then have been able to visualize all the speeches and proclamations being read on the stone balcony, nor to imagine the crowd gathered in front of the building to listen to the Declaration of Independence on July 18, 1776. This Old State House should remain here. Though its neighbourhood has all grown tall and grand, the streets that encircle the old structure are still narrow and twisted and not much different from what they used to be, and the people walking hereabouts are similar in look and gait, though not perhaps in costumes. I remember that Chicago once offered to buy the birthplace of Shakespeare from Stratford, England, to be put up on the shore of Lake Michigan, too. She might also have liked to buy Dante's house from Florence, Victor Hugo's house from Paris, or Confucius' Temple from Peking. What a great, unusual architect would have been needed to work out an amicable design for them all—not the late Mr. Frank Lloyd Wright, I presume. City designing is always confronted with a number of problems if old, historical buildings are to be preserved. However this problem was no concern of mine, so I went into the Old State House.

As I stepped up the stairs, a voice broke out suddenly: "It was up those stairs that Samuel Adams led his committee of fifteen to meet in the Council Chamber and to demand of the British Governor that 'all soldiery be forthwith removed from the towne.' " The words came from a person sitting at ease behind a desk on a slightly-raised platform. He spoke as if the words had come out of his mouth without him needing to raise his head to give me a look. I hardly realized that his words were addressed to me until I was looking at an oil painting and heard again: "Now you are standing where John Hancock was when he was inaugurated as the first Governor of the State in 1780. He had a blue silk waistcoat, embroidered in gold, inside his crimson velvet coat, with silk stockings and silver buckles on his pumps. His wife, Dorothy, was sitting not far away holding a small fan . . ." I still felt remote from the words, but no sooner did I stoop to look into a glass case than I heard: "You are now looking at wonderful cannon balls, big and small. Those wonderful cannon balls were made by the hands of Paul Revere. And the tankards, too. They are all solid silver. See that beautiful little tankard—Mrs. Revere liked it better than anything her husband made and kept it always. Here we value it highly, so we have a hidden lock and chain attached to it, in case . . ." There was no other visitor in the hall. The voice must have been addressing me. Yet the person who said all this still sat comfortably behind the desk without making a movement. He must have been the custodian of the house. His position being somewhat different from that of a museum guard or guide, he was naturally entitled to sit there while telling the tale. Also the room, or hall, is not big, and the words could be heard clearly from one corner to another. When I visited old houses in Paris, the old attendant would always relate some amusing anecdote about Madame Pompadour; in London the old-pensioner porter insisted on establishing whether he was in the Boer war or the first World War; in New York the young girl guide winked her eye from time to time while reciting about new buildings as there were no old ones to show; now in Boston the custodian just sat and related what was to be said. I have always said that human beings are fundamentally the same everywhere. So they are, but there can be surface differences.

On my way out of the Old State House I was still pondering over one of the exhibits. It was the horn of a unicorn, which had only recently come to light in a clearance of junk. Why the junk had not been cleared before is not for me to

Ch'i-lin
(Traditional Chinese unicorn)

ask. Nor is it necessary for me to know how the unicorn horn had come there. I know that the Unicorn is in the British Royal Ensign in company with the Lion. I understand that a unicorn is a mythical animal in Western mythology like its counterpart, Ch'i-lin or kylin, in China. The western unicorn is a white deer-like animal with a long ivory horn, while the Chinese ch'i-lin has a horse-like body covered with carp-like scales, a crest down the middle of the back, a bushy tail, cloven hoofs, and a head similar to the Chinese conventional dragon, with a short horn in the center of it like that of a rhinoceros. Unlike the Chinese dragon it does not make its appearance on earth very often; when it does, it is always regarded as an extremely good omen. On account of this, Ch'i-lin is a favourite subject for Chinese artists to mould in porcelain or carve in wood, ivory, and jade. There was a well-known story of this animal in connection with Confucius. When the old sage reached his seventies, he heard a unicorn being shot dead and sighed, saying: "Oh, Heaven, I am going to die!" The sudden appearance of the unicorn in the countryside startled the innocent people, for they did not know what it was in those early days of the sixth century B.C., so they rushed to kill it. As Confucious knew the unicorn to be a sacred animal, its unnatural death turned the extremely good omen of its appearance into a bad one and Confucius saw no more hope of putting the chaotic society of the decaying Chou dynasty into good order. He died not long afterwards. The famous Confucian scholar of the T'ang dynasty (618–906), Han Yü, wrote an essay to explain the capture of the Ch'i-lin which became a model for writing and was read by all the school boys and girls up to twenty years ago. Since its appearance in Confucius' late life, there has been no record of the reappearance of the Ch'i-lin in China. Perhaps there are no more Ch'i-lin in Heaven. The Ch'i-lin was made into an art object as one of the four sacred animals in the back design of Han and T'ang bronze mirrors. But I have found nothing about the unicorn horn in Chinese ancient books. I know very little about it in Western mythology. But from paintings, ensigns, and designs on tapestries I can see that its horn is a most prominent part of the animal, and must be a great treasure. I saw another unicorn horn in the Whitehills' home at North Andover. I have seen one in Oxford with an interesting story attached to it. Gladys and Van Wyck Brooks came to visit Oxford in May, 1951. The late H. N. Spalding of Brasenose College took us to see New College, founded in the fourteenth century and still called "New." The College Warden, Dr. A. H. Smith, former Vice-Chancellor of Oxford University, showed us their treasure room, which was not open to the public unless by special

arrangement. A white unicorn horn without the tip stood
in a corner of the room, and its story was told to us:

The College possessed a Unicorn's horn which was given
to it in the fifteenth century and which had been used until
the time of the Reformation as the shaft of a processional
cross. The cross was taken off at the time of the Reformation
in the middle of the sixteenth century, but the shaft was
kept as an object of value and interest.

It was shown in the later part of the sixteenth century to
Robert Dudley, the Earl of Leicester, who was at the time
Chancellor of the University of Oxford. The Earl was a
friend of Culpeper, who was Warden of New College, and
its virtue was explained to him. On his departure he said that
he would like to have the horn as a reminder of his happy
visit to the College. The Warden explained that this heir-
loom of the College could not be given away without reference to the Fellows, and after discussion with the Fellows a
compromise was arranged by which the Earl was given the
tip of the Horn. The rest of the Horn was kept back from
him, and the College still has its treasure without the tip.

The Earl was an influential person at the time, and a
compromise had to be made. But where the tip is now, no
one knows.

From the Old State House I found my way to Cornhill.
I read somewhere that there used to be a place called Back
Alley, which was so narrow that a tipsy-topsy man could not
fall to either side. The passage from Cornhill to Brattle
Street, with the Brattle Tavern on one side and the Brattle
Bookshop on the other, is quite narrow. I did not have a
drink in the Brattle Tavern even though I knew that I
would not be falling to either side of Brattle Street, but the

Brattle Bookshop had a visit from me more than once. It is a second-hand bookshop. Books, pamphlets, and magazines are there for the visitors to put in order. On my first visit I emerged from the back of the shop like a gold-miner full of gold dust.

Brattle Tavern

I then found the private street in Boston. The word *private* ahead of *street* interested me. It is called Bosworth St., and I reached it by a number of stone steps from Province Street. The street is not a private one. Boston, like London, always has something up her sleeve. She is unlike a modern supermarket and rather like a bazaar in any ancient land on earth. It is in Boston that one feels that one has never broken away from the old. In the old Granary Burying Ground I had already come on the names of Benjamin Franklin's parents, Paul Revere, Samuel Adams, Sewall, Otis, Hancock, and Faneuil. Now I came on Mother Goose. It not only surprised me, but shook me a great deal, for I realise that I should not have trusted what I learned without some

A private street is not private.

reservation. Trained in Mencius' thought of retaining one's childlike mind, after I arrived in England in 1933 I read many English nursery books to my young friends, daughters and sons of my big friends, before their bedtime, and I wrote a few storybooks for children. One of the most popular nursery rhymes that I heard was "Humpty Dumpty," but only now did I find out that Humpty Dumpty had his great fall from a wall in Pudding Lane, now called Devonshire Street of Boston. Pudding Lane is said to be where Mother Goose came to live with her daughter and son-in-law after the death of her husband, Issac Goose. I took many of my young friends in England to see the pantomime "Mother Goose" on the stage near Christmas time year after year. The heroine was always a huge goose, and I could never have imagined that she had been a real person. This proves how inscrutable the human mind can be. We are told to accept legends as legends and nothing more. Mother Goose was a traditional legend when I was living in England and will continue to be so. Yet now I learnt that Mother Goose was not a legendary figure but a proper Bostonian. Of course "Goose" is unusual as a family name, but there might be more unusual ones. It just so happened that Mother Goose had many songs and ditties to sing to her grandchildren all day long. If she lacked one or did not want to repeat she created a new one. Humpty Dumpty was her creation. But day after day her singing from dawn to dusk together with her following of young children drove her son-in-law nearly mad, for he, Thomas Fleet, was a peace-loving man and needed quietness to concentrate his mind on his ever-prosperous business as a printer. However, in those days of early Boston life, a son-in-law had to put up with his mother-in-law as in China. The wife was grateful to her mother for keeping an eye on the children. A modern wife would be, too. Yet a modern husband could not put up with the situation as Thomas Fleet did. Later the calculating Thomas Fleet printed the ditties of old Mother Goose for sale. He made good money and Mother Goose became a legendary figure. Thomas Fleet's resourcefulness of mind may have influenced all American minds ever since, for no American would turn down the most unlikely chance of making a gadget. The curious thing about it is that Mother Goose is more of a legend in England than in Boston or America at large. No doubt Issac Goose and his wife were either born in England or descended from English parents. But they had come to live in Boston. Why did the English never think of making known that the creator of Humpty Dumpty was a real Mother Goose of Boston?

During my stay in Boston I learnt to know two places where I could see the typical Boston men and women of today. At the northern end of Washington Street I noticed more than once a large number of people, mostly men and seldom women, standing on the edge of the pavement on either side and gazing at as well as murmuring the chalk words written on the boards of the Boston newspaper houses. This occurred between twelve and two o'clock on weekdays. Their stance, their moving lips, their smiles, and their arched eyebrows were all very interesting to watch. On the benches built against the wall on both sides of the Boston Public Library were mostly women, sitting there in the afternoons just watching the coming and going of cars and people in Copley Square. Young people were there too, but they were restive and very seldom sat. I found myself there several times. It was there I could study what the women wore, particularly in the way of flowery hats, in Boston some forty years or so ago. I, too, sat on the long bench with the rest, gazing and sketching the view of the old Trinity Church which blends so well with the Hancock building in the background. I only wished that fewer big touring coaches stopped by the green lawn in the center of the Square.

I was there again after my tour of Faneuil Hall, the Old State House, and Granary Burying Ground. The sky became darker when I reached there. Massive clouds hurried over us. The lighted top of the Hancock building seemed to have been dimmed. All of a sudden came a loud burst of thunder, followed by sharp lightning. Raindrops shot down in straight lines on the many people rushing in a panic. Some bumped into others; some sheltered wherever they thought it safe; and most of the crowd took refuge near the entrance of the Copley Square subway. I was one of the few to move slowly. I lingered to gaze at the scene, the excitement of which was not unusual in my experience in Boston. Boston rain differs from London's dramatically.

XI

Boston Ghosts

I N C H I N A the general belief is that everyone, on dying, becomes a ghost and lives again in much the same way as before but in a different world. We have ghost cries, ghost laughs, ghost walks, haunted spots, and, in short, all the ghostly "box of tricks" with which the superstitions are familiar all over the world. I remember that there were even ways of finding out what any particular ghost feared and taking precautionary measures. It seems natural that if spirits exist there must be both good and evil ones. The former give no trouble to anybody and in fact sometimes render assistance. But hideous devils infest dark corners, and lie in wait to injure unfortunate passers-by. The spirits of persons who have been wronged are especially dreaded by those who have done the wrong. I have heard and read many a story on this theme in my boyhood and they cautioned me not to do wrong to others. I thought it would be no fun to encounter the spirits of those who were wronged in their lifetime.

However, I decided to see the ghosts of three women who were hanged on Boston Common. I heard that pirates, Indians, murderers, thieves and highwaymen were hanged on the Common in the old days. None of their ghosts interested me, for they had deserved their fate. But Mary Dyer, Rachel Wall, and Margaret Jones were different.

Mary Dyer was a Quaker who came with William Robinson and Marmaduke Stevenson in September, 1659, to test the cruel laws that had been set up in Boston under Governor Endicott. Any Quaker who came to Boston was flogged and imprisoned with hard labor. They were banished upon the expiration of their sentences. Their ears were cut off if they returned. Their tongues were bored with a hot iron should they venture to return again with no ears. They were hanged if they insisted on making their return for the third time. On reading these words I sighed to myself, saying that these laws were exactly similar to the punishment of "a thousand cuts" of the Manchu dynasty of China, which today no longer deserves to be called the cruellest of all punishments in the whole history of mankind. On the 27th of October of 1659, Mary Dyer was dragged together with the other two, to the gallows on Boston Common under the guard of a hundred soldiers. Her two companions were hanged first. But Mary Dyer's son came to plead for her release, while the halter was placed on her neck. She was reprieved and left Boston with her son. Yet she returned the following spring refusing to go away again with the words, "In obedience to the will of the Lord I came and in His Name will I abide faithful unto death." So she accepted the unnatural death on Boston Common on June 1st, 1660. Though I am ignorant about the difference between a Quaker and other Christians, I know that "the thousand cuts" of the Manchu law were only applied to a most deadly criminal. I have found nothing to indicate that Mary Dyer was a deadly criminal.

Rachel Wall is said to have been very poor, yet she preached an idea in 1812 similar to what has been prevailing in Russia now. Nevertheless, being born a woman, she possessed an instinctive love of fancy head-wear, grabbed a beautiful bonnet from a lady's hand while strolling through the Common, and ran away with it. As a result she was hanged as a highway robber. The cost of the bonnet was about seventy-five cents.

Margaret Jones was the third woman in my list. She is known as the first woman doctor in America and produced a wonderful drug for her patients by mixing some aniseed with liquors. She cured untold numbers. Many more came to ask for her treatment and many more were cured. This went on, and in those days the people's minds soon questioned the nature of the treatment. She was suspected of possessing imps, was soon dubbed a witch, was tried and found guilty and was hanged on a strong branch of the biggest elm on Boston Common. Had she lived in these days of ours and cured so many patients she would have become a multimillionaire!

To me these three women were grossly wronged in their day. I thought their spirits would be still roaming round Boston Common at night, for in China in the past we believed that a spirit, if wronged, stayed in the place where the wrong was done. Therefore I roamed round the Common at night on many an occasion in the hope of seeing their spirits. I thought that if I could have a look at them, it might give me a clearer idea of the bygone days of Boston. Unfortunately none of them appeared to me. Perhaps the ghosts have found too many foreigners on the Common nowadays and have long left the city for the suburbs.

Once I was told that the ghost of Captain Kidd was still in Boston. This surprised me, for I knew he had been tried and executed in London. Being sent by the Colonial Governor of New England to catch pirates far away from Boston harbor, Captain Kidd did not return for years and was then rumoured to have become a notorious pirate himself. Finally he came back to report to his governor bearing much booty of jewels and gold as evidence of his struggle against pirates out at sea; but he was eventually arrested and locked up in Boston jail in 1700, thence transferred to London and executed. It would be an interesting study to find out how his ghost had crossed the Atlantic Ocean back to Boston from London.

I heard, too, that there used to be a ghost seen reading in the old Boston Athenaeum in Pearl Street, before it moved to Beacon Street in 1849. It was Dr. Harris's. In his lifetime he read there every day and long after his death he was seen reading there just the same by many people. I was urged to make sure of it by the present Director of the Boston Athenaeum, Walter Whitehill, who gave me a broad smile while stroking his impressive mustache and gently shaking his head.

In trying to see Boston ghosts I encountered many tales of devils, witches, and haunted houses in and around Boston. Cotton Mather's description of the devil as a tawny fellow and of the streets of Boston as reeking of brimstone interested me. As I have never seen a devil yet, I am unable to describe one, but according to Chinese books the devils in China were and are definitely Chinese. Cotton's tawny devil seemed not to be a Bostonian. Could he be an American Indian? It was possible and quite probable, for in the early Pilgrim period many Indians must have been seen in the streets of Boston. Their presence naturally filled the streets with brimstone. However of all the witches that Cotton Mather persecuted so cruelly and terribly, none were Indians. Neither of the Boston ghosts I heard of was tawny. The American Indians must have had their ghosts in the same way as we Chinese have ours, but none of their ghosts made their appearance or created a scene in and around Boston.

Sometime in 1947 or 1948 the late Strickland Gibson, then keeper of the Bodleian Library in Oxford, England, was arranging an exhibition of books and pictures on witchcraft throughout the world. The Bodleian is rich in early books and pictures to do with this subject in almost every country in Europe and also in Egypt, but has little information about it in the Middle East or China. Mr. Gibson asked me if I could suggest some book titles. My inadequacy was revealed. I do not claim that I know everything about China, but I could not remember reading anything comparable with the tales of witches, witchcraft and particularly the persecution of witches in Europe. On the other hand there must have been witches, for the word *wu*, which means "wizard" or "witch," has long been in the Chinese dictionary. On the oracle bones recently excavated from the ancient royal tombs dating back to the sixteenth century B.C. the word *wu* appears frequently in descriptions of what was done in divination in healing and in praying for rain.

Sorcerers existed in China from early days. They were active and quite important in ancient China when the ruler was in trouble with his health or with his state affairs. They were asked to perform their magical acts to dispel whatever caused the ruler to worry. Particularly in time of long drought, they were burned alive as sacrifice to the angry spirit in Heaven, so that rain might come. This practice was discontinued from the tenth century B.C. or perhaps earlier. Perhaps the fear of being burned alive prevented many people from taking to sorcery. However, burning-the-witch-alive to bring rain was in no way similar to the persecution of witches in Europe. Sorcerers or witches could never become a menace to the social structure of Chinese life under the domination of Confucius' teachings. Confucianism, with family life as the unit, left no opportunity for becoming a sorcerer except to those rare people who had no family life at all.

When I came to live in England in 1933, one of the many

things in Western life which interested me was the tales of witches and the ways in which they were persecuted. Though I could never bring myself to believe in the inhuman persecution, any more than Westerners can believe in the Chinese torture of a thousand cuts, I felt glad that I had arrived in Europe too late to see such persecution. Later I came to Boston and I heard and read that Boston and practically the whole of New England had undergone a similar stage of witch-persecution. This gave me a new interest, for the witches in Boston and New England had nothing to do with the native inhabitants. The early settlers had actually brought everything with them, including the fear of witchcraft—a wholesale, body-and-spirit exportation from England or a wholesale importation to America. Not only Captain Kidd's ghost, but witches, too, had crossed the ocean.

In the Pilgrim Period, Boston and New England everywhere seem to have been infested with witches. There was a haunted house in almost every town and village at a time. They have all vanished. Not even a slight trace of the footprint of Mother Cary, the witch, is to be found in Boston. However, friends suggested that I should go and see the Witch House or Ghost House that is still in existence in Salem. So I set off there one day.

To see the Witch House was not the sole object of my visit to Salem. I took a train on a June morning and arrived about ten-thirty. Walking along the platform under the tall, dim wall with a huge arch opening I felt that I was back somewhere inside Saint Pancras Station in London. The station building wore the English Gothic and Victorian air. It was the most impressive and striking architecture that had come my way in my travels in the United States.

Walking aimlessly, I came to a house on which a placard said "Ropes Memorial," built in 1719; I supposed the house

had belonged to the Ropes sisters, whose father sailed to
China specially to buy the youngest one tableware for a wed-
ding present. The house did not open until two o'clock, so
I moved on. My main purpose in visiting Salem was to see
the Essex Institute and the Peabody Museum, for both have

Witch House, Salem

many things from China, and also to visit The House of the
Seven Gables of which I read long ago.

In the Essex Institute I saw many original Salem witchcraft documents. The report of the original examination of
Martha Cory, who was hanged as a witch in 1692, was there,
together with the record in the handwriting of Rev. Samuel
Parris, attested by John Hathorne and Jonathan Corwin, the
witchcraft judges. I was told that in those days when Salem
was only a small town with seventeen hundred inhabitants,
hundreds were accused of witchcraft and many were hanged.
It was known as a witch-infested town. But Salem had her
glorious days several decades after the witchcraft trials. Most

of the Yankee skippers set off from Salem. All these sea-captains brought wealth back to the town.

A portrait of General Frederick Townsend Ward in the picture gallery of the Institute interested me. I had read about his services to the Manchu Imperial Government in quelling the rebel Chinese from the South. He was then only twenty-seven and led ten thousand Chinese soldiers to battle. They fought on land and sea and they were called "Chang-sheng-chün," or "ever-conquering legion." For three years he and the English Gordon were the foreign heroes of China. Unfortunately General Ward was shot in battle at Tz'u Hsi. After his death the Emperor had two temples built to his memory. It is said that soon his grave became a shrine, invested with miraculous power, and that Chinese came from far and wide to kneel down and pray there. Being a son of Salem, had General Ward inherited something of the old witchcraft and taken it with him to China, in the same way as the witchcraft of New England was brought over from the Mother Country? His uninterrupted winning of battles must have been attributed to miraculous power by the Chinese of the time. Therefore miraculous power can be one man's meat and another's poison. There is a book about the life of General Frederick Ward, called *A God from the West*. I know that I am wrong to speak of witchcraft and the General in the same breath, but I hope the descendants of his family, as well as the authorities of the Essex Institute, will not be angry with me, for I want to illustrate my point. In the old days each group of people lived far apart from one another and each could not see beyond his own boundary, and therefore their point of view was narrow and limited. Thus arose the terrible persecution of the witches. Had people's minds been broader a number of inhuman acts could have been avoided. The human mind has been widening all the time. I am glad to live in an age of broad-mindedness.

My admiration was also roused by the heroic behaviour of Mrs. Frederick Townsend Ward, a Chinese by birth. Her maiden name was Chang Meihua. Meihua means "Winter-plum blossom," a most prized flower in China, and her family name was Chang. Miss Chang met General Ward in Shanghai when he was a young soldier, and they married. After the general's death she came, still very young, to spend the rest of her days in the General's home at Chestnut Street. One can hardly imagine how Salem society came to accept her, for in those days it must have been rare for an American to marry a Chinese. I can imagine how much she herself battled against her love for the General, not wishing to distress her strictly Confucian parents. I think she must have been very well-brought-up, otherwise she could not have surmounted the prejudices of the narrow-minded Salem society of the time and established herself in it. It is said that she always decked her head and body with sparkling jewels and jades and wore satin gowns embroidered with bats and sapphire butterflies. To those who befriended her she looked fine, but to some she may well have seemed a witch. Fortunately her husband had been a General in the Chinese Imperial service, a foreign hero for the Chinese and a source of pride for the Americans, so she was made welcome at least superficially by the women of Salem. However, she could not have gained her position in Salem society had she not behaved in exemplary fashion. Had she innocently talked about the embroidered "bat" on her satin gown as a symbol of happiness, without explaining that the Chinese words for "bat" and "happiness" have the same sound, many women of Salem might have thought she was trying to bewitch them. She has won my admiration for her loyalty to her love and for the way in which she upheld the high esteem of the Chinese by her behaviour in a foreign country. Chang Meihua of Salem should be made known to all Chinese.

I must also take off my hat to the authorities of the Essex Institute, who are said to have refused a blank-check offer from the Library of Congress for the portrait of Alexander Hamilton that is still hanging in their portrait gallery. After all, not all Yankees are money-minded.

When I came down from the library of the Institute, a lady told me to follow the guide into the courtyard. After having paid my fee, I managed to move about the John Ward House without the guide's attention. The "Penny Shop" interested me. Lying on the desk were a number of penny books in very small print on natural history, insects, birds, and animals; the size of each book was about one and a half inches by two and a half inches. There were many other little things, and upstairs was full of junk, dress models, dummies, trunks, drug bottles, and weaving tools. The early settlers from old England knew how to do everything themselves. By the side of John Ward House, which was said to have been built in 1684, was a very small "Old Cobbler's Shop," inside which could stand one person only.

My first visit to the Peabody Museum took place after lunch that day. Now I made a tour of the front room, where many big models of ships and things belonging to ships were beautifully displayed. Then I went to see the Chinese room, which was full of Chinese bric-a-brac that had been brought back by the sea-captains in the China Trade period. There is also a pair of big Chinese porcelain bowls in the shape of ducks, together with two impressive life-size models of Chinese merchants in the costume of the Manchu period. While visiting the Japanese room, where the display was richer and better arranged, and then the upper balconies where China was represented on one side and Asia—including India,

Cambodia, and Burma—on the other, I overheard two young girls talking in front of a Siamese Buddha statuette. One remarked, "Those people worship him," and the other answered, "They don't now. That is natural." I felt that the word "natural" slipped out of the girl's mouth naturally and showed that they must have been taught to think that way in school.

My attention was next devoted to the natural-history rooms. My weak point is that I just cannot keep away from objects coming from Nature. I have been to a few museums of natural history, the best of which are the one in New York and the one in Chicago, but I was always amazed and confused by the many things to see in the big museums that I often overlooked interesting points. In the Natural History rooms of Peabody Museum I became interested in two things. One was the parti-colored American lobster, found in Beverly Harbor in 1930 and the other, the enormous claw of a lobster weighing thirty pounds, which was caught by someone of Gloucester. There were a number of abnormal lobster claws on show and the explanation was that "injury to lobster claws during the short periods of growth when the lobster is soft-shelled often results in curious abnormalities." One of the thirty different kinds of abnormalities I saw was two claws growing on one stem, one small and the other big, both with teeth. I remember seeing a big claw in the shape of a human head in the harbor of Provincetown; it seemed like the chin of the English actor, Jack Hulbert. I made a sketch of it.

The other thing I learned was that the American bison is an immigrant from Asia which arrived during one of the several periods when Siberia was connected by land with Alaska. Yet there is no trace of it at all in Asia. When the Chinese began to domesticate the buffalo for ploughing the rice fields is still unknown. The Chinese buffalo is a very docile, harmless creature, while its African counterpart is wild and fearful. The American bison seems to stand in between.

Recently the museum was sent an ornament made from the bones of the fabulous moa bird by a member of their ethnological expedition to New Zealand and the Cook Islands, which set out to study the Polynesians. I was interested to learn that the moa was a bird so large in size that one variety of it, larger than a man, stood ten to twelve feet high, while the smallest was about four and a half feet high. Many skeletons of them have been found in Pyramid Valley, New Zealand. The moas are thought to have been roaming New Zealand in large numbers when the first settlers arrived there from Tahiti about one thousand years ago. It is said that they were abundant there two million years back. This recalls to my mind the following passage from *Chuang Tzu,* a book written by one of the great Chinese philosophers, Chuang Tzu, in the third century B.C.

In the south there is a bird. It is a kind of phoenix. Do you know it? When it starts from the South Sea to fly to the North Sea, it does not alight except on the wu-t'ung tree. It eats nothing but the fruit of the bamboo, drinks nothing but the purest spring water. An owl which had got the rotten carcass of a rat, looked up as the phoenix flew by, and screeched.

Chuang Tzu may have heard of the moa, for New Zealand lies south of China. The only difference is that the moa was a great walking, flightless bird. Perhaps, Chuang Tzu, having himself not seen the bird, thought such a large winged creature must be able to fly fast and far. Though my deduction may sound far-fetched, it is interesting to know that in the ancient days, knowledge of strange, unusual things did travel from one place to another in spite of the great distances. It seems that the knowledge of our modern man is far behind the times—two thousand years had to pass before we knew of the existence of the moa.

The Peabody Museum of Salem is a center of Polynesian studies. There are many Polynesian exhibits in the showcases, and the library is rich in books on Polynesia.

Having spent quite a time in the Museum that day, I left for a stroll on the waterfront. After a glance at the Hawthorne statue at one end of Hawthorne Boulevard, I walked along Orange Street and soon found myself on Derby Wharf. A signboard read:

Derby Wharf: center of Salem shipping 1760–1860. Base for Privateering in the revolution and in the war of 1812. Vessels sailed from here on pioneering voyages to distant parts of the world.

So up to a hundred years ago, Derby Wharf was a center of American trade with west and east. There must have been countless ships lying in the harbor and along the piers. Now, in front of my eyes, the seawater was rippling gently as if nothing had ever happened in this corner. The past is past, yet who knows where the ripples may end. Confucius once said that the wise took pleasure in flowing water. From it we gain a sense of continuity and learn that new things keep deriving from the old. Thus one becomes wiser. Derby Wharf was a wharf no more, but a high sandy bank with green grass growing on it. That afternoon it was quite warm, and the bright sun still shone on the few who sat or lay on the grass. None seemed to be wanting to say anything. After a look at the water flowing along the edge of the wharf, I walked idly back, gazing occasionally at the solitary building of the old Custom House of Salem, where Hawthorne worked miserably. I reached the building but could not get in to see the Hawthorne room. I did not mind. Hawthorne was there no more. However, Hawthorne will outlive the

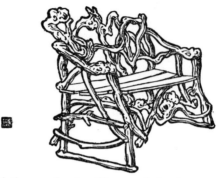

An artistic seat in the House of the Seven Gables

existence of Derby Wharf in years to come, I guess. Words have a more lasting effect than material objects.

At last I sat down to rest on a rough-hewn but artistic-looking bench in the garden yard of the House of Seven Gables. Far ahead of me was the water of the harbor. I was thinking that Hawthorne must have sat on this very seat sometimes when his mind was working on the happenings inside the house. My mind at the moment was recalling the description of the house in the novel. Then I got up to join a group that a smartly dressed young woman was showing round. At a certain point I noticed that the young guide was forgetting what she had read in the novel. From that moment I felt that I had the advantage of Hawthorne as far as the interior arrangement of the house was concerned. When he visited the house, it was still occupied by a large family. He could not have been taken into the women's chambers to explore every corner and to be shown what was underneath a bed-cover as we visitors were. On the other hand, no family with youngsters could have kept the rooms so spotlessly clean, no matter how many domestic helpers the owner had. Hawthorne did not manage to see half of the house properly, I can be sure. A friend of mine told me jokingly that the House of Seven Gables had only five gables originally—the extra two were added by a hand with miraculous power overnight. That hand belonged to Hawthorne. I suggested that Hawthorne might have chosen the word "seven" instead of "five" for the rhythm of the sound as well as to indicate that he was writing fiction. One thing inside the house is the secret staircase by the fireplace and round the chimney. Directly after the words "secret staircase" were pronounced, an elderly lady exclaimed romantically and excitedly that she had always dreamed about a secret staircase and now she had the opportunity to walk on one. Her grown-up children who were with her said nothing. The guide then had something to say about the secret staircase. It served a three-fold purpose, to hide from the witch, to hide slaves from being taken away, and to hide treasures which the sea-captain owners brought back from the Orient. Suddenly the same elderly lady spied the door with two different door-hinges. The guide explained that one type of hinge was to prevent evil spirits entering through the crack of the door.

The mention of "witch" sent me back to see the Witch House at 310½ Essex Street, which I had passed on my way. It was still closed to visitors, and it did not seem to have been open to the public for some time.

Crossing Mystic Bridge with David McCord on rainy night

Rain falls as forever,
Wind rushes,
And clouds become dense.

The new Mystic Bridge
Shows not its shape,
Yet is full of pulsing sound.
Close by all is dark and obscure;
Far away myriads of lights wink.
Happily together a poet and I,
 talking about the old and the modern,
And laughing at the ups and downs of the human
 world,
Are heading towards the heart of Heaven:
Lo, thousands and thousands of bright lamps,
Rows and rows of yellow gold!

XII

Boston Mouth

Don't eat with your ears;" wrote Yuan Mei, an eight-eenth-century Chinese poet and writer whose cookery-book is as famous and popular as his poems, "by which I mean do not aim at having extraordinary out-of-the-way foods, just to astonish your guests; for that is to eat with your ears, not with the mouth." "Don't eat with your eyes;" again said he, "by which I mean do not cover the table with innumerable dishes and multiply courses indefinitely. For this is to eat with the eyes, and not with the mouth."

During my stay in Boston I found Boston mouth func-tioning properly of its own accord.

It is difficult nowadays to enter any big city in Europe or America without being told that such-and-such restaurants serve good food. I have accustomed myself to eat with my ears, just to hear these names first before I made use of my mouth. After arrival in a city I have usually made calls on friends who then often made me eat with my eyes at attrac-tive restaurants with courteous service. It was always a grati-fying occasion for me, but not easy for me in such circum-stances to see how the mouth of the place functioned. Though I am no expert on food and wine and cannot say much about either, I have been struck by the proper func-tioning of the Boston mouth. Boston is perhaps the only city in America to have its name attached to a number of foods which, Yuan Mei would say, should neither be eaten with the ears nor with the eyes. They are Boston beans and cod, Boston clam chowder and Boston fish chowder.

So far my Boston friends have not given me Boston beans and cod to taste. There is still this happy moment in store for me in Boston. However, I had my first taste of Boston clam chowder on Fishermen's Wharf in San Francisco. After a month's stay in Boston, without having had Boston clam chowder, I moved to the west coast. With Boston fresh in my memory I particularly chose this dish when I was taken to Fishermen's Wharf for San Francisco crab. When I returned to Boston and remarked on the fine bowl of Boston clam chowder I had had in San Francisco, my friends did not even raise their eyebrows, they just let my words pass unnoticed. This puzzled me. Sometime afterwards one of the members of a dinner party asked me if I thought the food in Boston Chinatown genuine. I nodded my head, saying that I understood what he meant by Boston clam chowder in San Francisco.

It was in Marblehead that I must have had a genuine bowl of Boston clam chowder. Mr. Ernest Dodge, Director of the Peabody Museum of Salem, took me and three other members to lunch at the Boston Yacht Club. At that lunch I learned that Boston clam chowder is far superior to New York clam chowder. Colonel George Smith declared the New York brand unworthy of the name. My host joked that there was so much tomato and other vegetables in New York clam chowder that the eaters could only guess at the genuineness and freshness of the shell-fish.

There is another kind of chowder, quahog chowder, which only exists in Boston and has finely-chopped clams in the chowder. I learned the nature of this bowl from its name, *quahog*, of Indian origin, but I found no such word as chowder in the Oxford dictionary.

After having had dinner at the Blue Ship Tea Room at

the end of T-Wharf, I was introduced to the taste of the Boston fish chowder at Jimmy's Harbour Side Restaurant on Northern Avenue. I had welcomed the suggestion to sample it, for I thought any dish to do with fish must be good in Boston, where cod is always being mentioned and which has been a fishing center on the east coast of America for two or three hundred years. Boston does know how to use her fish, and the bowl of fish chowder I had was good. In our conversation my friend assured me that the fish in the chowder was cod, but that other types of fish could be used. The fish consumed in Boston comes chiefly from the sea, not from the fresh water of rivers or lakes. In China I only knew fresh-water fish dishes. I don't remember having anything like fish chowder in China. If chowder is an Indian dish by origin, I must admit that the early American Indians were not quite the same as the Chinese in their eating habits, though I always maintain that we both had the same origin. Of course, cooking varies from place to place even in China, and the early American Indians cooked what they could find locally.

A busy morning walking round the North End of Boston gazing at different historical places and squeezing through the marketing throng in Adams Square for two or three hours made me feel a little weary. I needed something to strengthen my limbs. I soon joined a long queue outside a door leading to a restaurant, the only one I could find in that quarter. Nor did I try to find another, for I thought there wouldn't be so many people waiting here if there were other eating places nearby. While queueing I revisualized the route of my wanderings. I then remembered hearing that a dish of pie is still traditional on all New England break-fast tables. To have pie for breakfast does not surprise a Chinese, for we can have anything we fancy in the early morning, provided it is handy and easy to prepare. But when I mentioned this tradition to an English friend of mine, he remarked that it had originated locally and had nothing to do with the mother country. A Boston friend told me to watch at hotel dining tables for those who chose pie for breakfast. They could only be Bostonians or New Englanders.

Another tradition in Boston is to have baked beans for Saturday night supper. On hearing of beans we Chinese would think either of soya beans, which produce the soya sauce now universally used in America, or small green beans, which are used to produce bean sprouts for many kinds of dishes in Chinese restaurants. But the Boston baked beans are different. I was told that the dried beans should be soaked overnight, and then parboiled for a while the next morning, before being poured together with salt pork, dry mustard, salt, treacle, pepper and some water into a big crockery pot to be baked at low heat for a whole day. It is apparently better to let the beans boil dry now and again in order to give them a rich brown colour.

At last I found myself at the head of the queue and entered the restaurant. I took a seat opposite a big marketman in a white overall, who was beginning to shove in one big mouthful after another from a mountainlike dish. He did not raise an eye to look at me. I picked up the menu, which gave me the name of the restaurant, Durgin-Park, and had two lists of dishes, "Dinner Bill" and "Supper Bill." I was puzzled that there was nothing labelled "lunch." A buxom, lively woman called to me to look under "Dinner Bill." She soon brought me a big plate with two huge slices of roast beef and many other things on it. By the time I had eaten the first slice my eagerness for food was damped. My opposite number got up, still paid no heed to me, and went away. The

Salem Custom House

Faneuil Hall

waitress came to clear the place for the next customer, an exceptionally tall fellow. She then looked at my plate and said: "What's the matter, young man? Can't you finish your plateful? If you can't, you should not have come here to waste your money; if you don't like the food, we want to know why. We don't like people who don't like our food. You must have seen the line-up outside." She ended with a good laugh and I knew she meant it all as a joke. But the situation embarrassed me. My excuse was that my appetite had been reduced by the food-rationing in England during the war and afterwards. Her eyes brightened and became round: "So you have just come from England. Then you can finish this." An enormous bowl of strawberry shortcake was thrust in front of me. I love strawberries and I felt that I was obliged to finish the big bowlful. I managed.

With David McCord I have been lucky to see a great deal of the proper functioning of Boston mouth. One evening we dined at Locke-Ober's and had a hearty meal of Roast-beef-and-Yorkshire-pudding, though their best-known specialties are American and French dishes. Afterwards I indulged in eating with my eyes, and I thought Yüan Mei would have forgiven me. I found the look of the room very English; the shiny brass nails on the leather-backed chairs as well as the bright brasses on the walls reminded me of the old London Art Club in St. James's Street near Piccadilly Circus. The most striking feature in Locke-Ober's for the feast of eyes is a Rubens type of fleshy nude hanging in the middle of the wall. It was brightly lit by a fluorescent light. My host could not say how long it had hung there nor how if had come to be there. I remembered reading an account of a debate on the acceptance of Bacchante in the Centennial History of the Boston Public Library and in *The Vicissitudes of Bacchante in Boston,* both by Walter Muir Whitehill. On

July 16, 1896, a reduced model of Bacchante came to the Art Commission of the City of Boston for approval and it at once roused great controversy for many considered that "The statue would undoubtedly shock a great many people. . . . The statue . . . was that of a drunken woman" as General

Bacchante once in Boston
Public Library since 1880

Bacchante in Boston
Art Festival since 1970

Francis A. Walker, President of M.I.T., objected, adding that "there would be a want of sympathy between it and its surroundings." This kept the Boston journalists and cartoonists busy for days. On Sunday evening, November 22 of the same year, the Reverend James B. Brady preached to an audience of two thousand five hundred on the theme, "Treason in the Boston Public Library." "Away with the horrid thing, and bury it where the Bostonians buried the tea in

1773," while the Congregational Club announced: "the statue is not simply nude, it is glaringly and obtrusively naked, it is an offence to the temperance sentiment of the community." Though it had many admirers, the statue was removed and is now housed in the Metropolitan Museum of Art, New York City. On account of this I felt sure that the Rubens-type, though artistically good perhaps, could not have made its appearance in Locke-Ober's while Bacchante was being attacked. Boston is not the only place where such a controversy has occurred. I have learned that when Velazquez's "Reclining Nude" was shown in the National Gallery of London for the first time two Victorian-minded ladies secretly slashed it with a penknife, though the cuts were repaired and are invisible. There was also the sensation created by the picture "September Morn" in New York some forty years ago. All these incidents reveal to me that the whole world, Western or Eastern, is of one mind. Confucius' teachings center on the *Moral Law of Man,* which dominates the Chinese mind above anything. Life study has been impracticable in Chinese artistic training and there has never been a nude painting in the annals of Chinese painting. In my Phi Beta Kappa Oration on "The Chinese Painter" delivered at Harvard University on 11th June 1956, I have the following passage:

At the beginning of the twentieth century, Chinese students began to go abroad to acquire modern knowledge. . . . What they brought back were a few cheap plaster of Paris casts of Western sculptures and a number of badly reproduced prints. By exhibiting these with their own works in oil, pencil and chalk —and exhibitions of any kind were then a very new thing in China—they made a big stir, comical as it may sound now. They attached great importance to the study of nudes, and this at once raised strong opposition from the ardently Confucian-minded. A warrant was issued for the arrest of one returned traveller from Paris who had managed to find one live model for his newly established art school in Shanghai.

Unfamiliarity provokes human instincts but provocation loses ground when unfamiliarity becomes familiarity. Nobody has ever asked whether the works by modern abstract artists exhibited now in the Massachusetts Insitute of Tech-

Geometric MIT

nology are in sympathy with their surroundings. Actually not one of the diners in Locke-Ober's except myself lifted his head to feast his eyes on the nude painting. Boston mouth functioned there properly indeed.

In Oyster Union House, near North Station, to which I was taken by Dr. Miyawakee Scott of Boston University, I found myself being rejuvenated. Directly after we sat down we were each given a paper apron to tie round our necks. There was a big lobster printed in bright red in the center of it and its shape was very similar to the aprons made of linen or silk with designs of a Chinese lion or butterflies and flowers in the center, that a young Chinese child would wear. I must have worn such an apron when I was very young, though I could not claim to know what was on it. Now I met the lobster design in my fifth decade. While eating, my mind went back to some fresh lobsters I had when I stayed at the house of Mr. and Mrs. Wendell S. Hadlock by Chickawaukee Lake. Wendell, director of the William A. Farnsworth Museum at Rockland, said to me that the people of Maine are never at a loss as to what to offer a guest to eat—lobsters of course.

I am rejuvenated

I have, however, never been on more than nodding-acquaintance terms with oysters. I am in no position to compare myself with Thackeray, so I have no confession to make as to whether I felt "as if I had swallowed a small baby" on swallowing oysters in Boston's Parker House. I have enjoyed Parker House rolls a few times. On one occasion there I felt exhilarated inside after noticing the name of an unusual dish—I mean, unusual in that I had never seen such a dish in all my twenty or so years of residence outside China. It was "codfish tongues and cheeks sauté" and I ordered it with a smile at my host. Many kinds of freshwater fish cooked in the Chinese manner are served complete with head, for we Chinese consider the fish cheek, brain and tongue the most delicious parts of the whole. They are soft and tender and each has a flavour of its own. The cooking of them depends on the factor of timing. The dish I had that day was wonderful beyond words. I don't remember ever seeing fish tongues and cheeks served alone in China. In England the fishmonger finds cod-heads unsalable. Boston cod prepared in Boston hotels and restaurants is good, but the "codfish tongues and cheeks sauté" can only be had at Boston's Parker House.

It seems to me a fact that Americans are more used to foreign food, including Chinese food, than are the English. Nevertheless, there is a difference in the American regard for Chinese food and the food of other countries. I do not mean that they prefer Chinese food. But I think that, though they may have been familiar with Chinese food for years either in China or in America, they do not always seem to be sure of what they have eaten, when they come to order the same dish again. The obstacle is the Chinese names of the dishes and the difficulty increases when the southern people of China, mostly Cantonese, insist on printing the names in the transliteration of their local dialect rather than in what is known as the Chinese national language or Peking dialect. When no Chinese characters are attached to the names of the dishes, not only are those Americans who have been in China and learned the Chinese language puzzled, but also many Chinese not born in southern China. I, for one, have always found difficulty with the names of Chinese dishes which friends expected me to translate for them. As a rule I give a brief speech on the nature of the Chinese language, which does not help to interest the eaters in the food, but instead makes them resolve not to learn the names of the dishes. I am sure that no Frenchman would have to give a talk on the French language in a French restaurant. Nor will a Frenchman be asked to suggest which French restaurant in Boston is the best as I was asked to do in the case of Chinese restaurants almost as soon as I had arrived in the city. I felt that I must quickly visit a number of Chinese restaurants. Being unable to converse freely with the proprietors in their local dialect, my feeling towards the names of the dishes was the same as that of my American friends, though it did not prevent me enjoying the food. My personal opinion is that Chinese food in the Chinese restaurants is good and that its quality is about the same in all of them. Perhaps all the Chinese restaurateurs have a mutual understanding to avoid competition which might baffle the would-be consumer still more. It is surely fun to switch one's taste to Chinese dishes once in a while just as I have tried Boston clam chowder, Boston fish chowder, Durgin-Park's strawberry shortcake, Parker House rolls and Parker House codfish tongues and cheeks sauté.

George Caspari insisted on taking me to dine at an unusual place in Boston. Though his office is in New York, his business brings him over to Boston occasionally. We managed to fix a date and a special arrangement was made. Having a cocktail at Miss Bergerud's apartment first, the three of us then went downstairs. There we were greeted by two gentlemen in white aprons. The one with a white cap on his head held several academic degrees. I was introduced. The other was formerly an architect doing a good business in Boston for a number of years. There were five tables in the room, and thirty people could dine at one time if necessary. But they do not want to cater so many if they can help it. A dinner order has to be arranged long ahead, and only three evenings in the week are open for service. As Miss Bergerud is their friend, we were lucky to be there all by ourselves. The dinner was scrumptious, particularly the thick, tender, and juicy steak which came from Chicago by air every week. My eyes already moved round the room once. It is like a dinning hall of an old English home. But the pictures, maps, plates and other antique pieces hanging on the walls are not all English. The tables, chairs, and lamps represent the colonial days; some came from the Caribbean islands. What impressed me most was the fine set of thirty or forty pieces of pewter in different sizes as if they were made at the same time. They were collected from different places at an interval of many years. We had coffee in a small living room and sank ourselves in easy armchairs. The two white-apron gentlemen joined the conversation. They were experimenting what they could do by themselves at their own will after they had been working under others for years. They seemed to have succeeded. Three or four days' work in the week leave them enough time for their own pleasure in reading, going to concerts and hunting for antiques. In summer they would close the place and go to South America or some other places for vacation. In the fall they return to resume the experiment. It has no name but is at No. 9, Knox Street, Boston. I enjoyed the food, the conversation more and the atmosphere most.

No special Boston brewery had come to my notice. Yet I was told that a common function of Boston mouth has long been heavy drinking. The Boston merchants of 1763 estimated that about a million gallons of rum were consumed in Massachusetts every year, an average of four gallons per head. But those who lived in Boston and its neighbourhood drank the lion's share. The population of Boston has increased enormously since 1763, and I am assured that the amount of rum consumed per head per year has not decreased. I can see that the figure for the number of gallons consumed now must be a startling one.

Incidentally, I learned that one of the best rare-vintage judges in America was a Boston man, the late Mr. Charles Codman—nothing could be more appropriate than the

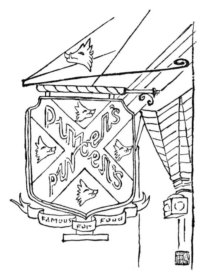

Famous for food

name. My friend wanted to take me to see him; an arrangement could not be made, for I had to leave Boston for San Francisco at the time. Perhaps it was better for him that I did not go to bother him, for I am no experienced drinker, much less a wine-connoisseur. Mr. Codman has declared about wine-tasting: "There is really nothing scientific to wine-tasting. It is all a matter of memory. The whole secret is being able to remember how a previous wine tasted. There are established tastes to certain wines, and if there is difference, this change must be noted."

I suppose this memory palate plays its part where food is

concerned too. Those who can distinguish a good dish from a less good one must be able to remember how a similar dish previously tasted. Chinese restaurants in Boston Chinatown need to be frequented if one is to create established tastes for certain dishes. In the same way I shall miss no chance of tasting Boston clam chowder, Boston fish chowder, etc. It is nowadays very difficult to secure domestic help and a cook at home, but I am sure that nothing in the annals of the function of Boston mouth has ever matched the following story which is recorded in Yuan Mei's Cookery book:

When I was at Peking there was a certain gentleman who was very fond of inviting guests, but the food was not at all good. One day a guest said to him, "Do you count me as a good friend?" "Certainly I do," said the host. The guest then knelt in front of him, saying, "If you are indeed my friend, I have a request to make to you, and I shall not rise from my knees till it is granted." "What is your request?" asked the astonished host. "That you will promise," said the guest, "that in future when you ask people to dinner, you will not ask me."

XIII

Boston China

B o s t o n C h i n a is not the same sort of term as Chelsea china or Dresden china. There should be a short dash between the two words, to indicate that the first does not qualify the second but that they are happily connected. In the past their connection was through trade—the China trade; at present it is through cultural associations, particularly through the Asiatic Department of the Boston Museum of Fine Arts, Fogg Museum and the Harvard-Yenching Institute.

To my horror I immediately made a serious blunder in connection with Boston and China, due to my habit of not reading about a place before I visit it. Being born in the country where the tea leaf was first used to make a beverage and having been used to English afternoon tea and tea parties for many years, a chance mention of the Boston *Tea Party* drew from me the remark that I would like to join it. Next morning a small headline appeared in the *Christian Science Monitor* stating "Our Chinese visitor came to Boston Tea Party 168 years too late."

If tracing back is to be done, then China must be blamed for using tea as a beverage. Perhaps not China as a whole but the Chinese who first discovered tea to be good for drinking. But who was he? Does any Chinese know? Definitely not I. I have only read that tea was praised by Chinese poets in the fourth century. The following passage from the book *Tea Leaves* by Francis S. Drake interests me:

Dr. Holmes, the annalist, says, tea began to be used in New England in 1720. Small quantities must, however, have been made many years before, as small copper tea-kettles were in use in Plymouth in 1702. The first castiron tea-kettles were made in Plympton, (now Carver), Mass., between 1760 and 1765. When ladies went to visiting parties, each one carried her tea-cup, saucer, and spoon. The cups were of the best china, very small, containing about as much as a common wine-glass.

The last sentence touches me very closely, for I come from the very city in China where these cups must have been made. The description suggests the exact type that has been used and is still in use in China now. These cups, made of the best china, must have come from the kilns at Ching-te-Chen, a manufacturing town in the district Fou-liang, not far from my birthplace, Kiukiang. The kilns were set up in Ching-te-Chen long before the tenth century, as soon as Chinese potters discovered the virtue of the local clay. The town however, did not receive its present name until 1004 in the beginning of the reign of Ching-te. Most of the best china was made there. But Ching-te-Chen lies inland and is surrounded by hills and mountains. The products had to be sent to Kiukiang, a city of historical and commercial importance on the south side of the Yangtse River between Shanghai and Hankow, for transportation in all directions. By degrees most china manufacturers had a center in Kiukiang, where they displayed their goods. The official residence of the former Imperial supervisors of K' and Hsi (1662–1722) and Ch'ien Lung (1736–1795) periods used to be in the city of Kiukiang, though the headquarters were in Ching-te-Chen. One of my great-great-uncles was connected with the Imperial supervisor's office. My father, being a trained artist in the Chinese tradition, used to do designs and himself painted plates and large-sized porcelain screens.

It was his pride to finish a set of porcelain screens, usually a landscape design with figures, and to see them treasured in the home of an art collector and connoisseur. When young I learned from father the technique of painting on porcelain and I still do it sometimes for friends and for myself for fun. I cannot of course claim that my family had any direct connection with those tea-cups used by the Boston ladies in the eighteenth century. Since I came to live in England in 1933, I have been repeatedly asked why Chinese tea-cups are so small and have no handles. The reason is that the best Chinese tea is to be sipped, not to be gulped, and that we hold the cup encircled by one hand, sometimes by both hands, not only to keep our hands warm in winter but to show how fond we are of our tea. The Chinese only drink hot tea. Ice tea is an American innovation. Apparently, the fashion of carrying their tea-cups about did not persist long among Boston ladies, if we are to believe the following lines written in 1773, by Susannah Clarke, Warrington's great-grandmother's sister. By then, non-tea-drinking was held to be a religious duty by American women:

> We'll lay card and wheel,
> And join our hands to turn and reel;
> We'll turn the tea all in the sea,
> And all to keep our liberty.

> We'll put on home-spun garbs,
> And make tea of our garden herbs;
> When we are dry we'll drink small beer,
> And FREEDOM shall our spirit cheer.

I was amazed to find that tea, drunk from small Chinese tea-cups, could have so much to do with *liberty* and *freedom*.

People in the West have all heard from one source or another of the tea-ceremony in the East, but very few realise that the tea-ceremony is now solely a Japanese affair. Not even those who went to see the popular play or movie *Teahouse of The August Moon* realised this. Actually, the ceremony of the tea-drinking contest was introduced by the men of letters of the Sung dynasty (960–1278), and in that period a special type of porcelain for tea-cups was produced in Fukien Province. It eventually became known to us as *Chien-yao*. It has a dark brownish black glaze with silver thread inside. The Japanese treasure this type of Chinese porcelain more than other people and they have a special name for it, *Tehmoku*. During the Sung period many Japanese came to study in China and they took back with them the Chinese ceremony of the tea-drinking contest. By degrees, Japanese thought and belief influenced the ceremony, which became more elaborate and became solely a Japanese festival which they call *Cha-no-yu*. After the Sung period China was ruled by Mongolian rulers, beginning with Kublai Khan. The Mongolians drank goat's milk—they did not care much for tea—and the tea-drinking contest gradually lost ground and soon disappeared in China.

This link between Boston and China established by the Boston Tea Party was a chance one. Boston established its direct connection with China through the China trade soon after the revolution. Of course no Chinese can claim to have a part in the making of America in the first stage of her history, but through the China trade many Bostonian families laid the foundations of wealth, which was to enable them to foster enterprises that are still flourishing throughout America today. Before 1773 the British trade laws obliged the colonists to secure all Oriental commodities by way of England. A month after Congress ratified the peace agreement with England, American ships began to go abroad independently in search of trade. No part of the world could offer richer and better rewards to the American traders than China. The first American vessel to reach Canton was the *Empress of China,* which sailed from New York on February 22, 1784, with Major Samuel Shaw of Boston on board. In Canton, Major Shaw acted as honorary American Consul and died on his return journey from the east in 1794 at the age of thirty-nine. Perhaps I may say that the Chinese owe Major Shaw much for the firm friendship between America and China which was launched by his stay in Canton. Had more Americans like Major Shaw of Boston gone to China subsequently, the relations between the two countries could have been even better.

In those early days of America the Yankees had little to offer for sale to the Chinese except a kind of herb that grew wild in the woods of New England. The roots of this herb, called by the Chinese ginseng, had long been known to have medicinal properties and had been prescribed in the ancient Chinese medical books. Its Latin name is *aralia quinquefolia.* Its root often takes the shape of a human body. It grows in Manchuria but not elsewhere in China. Owing to its rarity and its supposed strengthening and tonic properties it has been much sought by old and well-to-do people; it commands a high price. My grandmother used to boil this root and then drink the liquid in which it had boiled. Chinese ginseng is more expensive than the foreign-grown herb, which has chiefly come from Korea and America. So my grandmother was one of the consumers of American ginseng.

However, the sale of American ginseng alone could not have sustained the China trade for long. Soon those adventurous Boston merchants discovered that the Chinese would pay high prices for the lustrous pelts of the sea-otters and seals from the Pacific Northwest coast of America. They made deals with the local Indians for large consignments of these pelts in exchange for blankets, shoes, nails, chisels, gimlets, and beads. Then the *Columbia* sailed in 1788 with the first cargo of pelts westwards around stormy Cape Horn and northwards up the Pacific coast to Canton, where the pelts were sold at a great profit. Apparently the chisels exchanged with the Indians, one chisel for one pelt, were of the cheapest sort and could be made right on the ship; and on the Canton market each skin would fetch fifty American dollars. It is little wonder that the China-trade grew rapidly and that the connection between Boston and China became most friendly. I do not know exactly why the pelts of the sea-otter were so prized in China, but I guess that most of them must have been used for winter clothes. Except in Canton, which is in a semi-tropical zone and not cold in winter, China can be very cold for several months. The Chinese have long lined their winter clothes with furs such as yak, sheep, lamb, fox, sea-otter and seal. If only a tiny fraction of the vast population used sea-otter and seal it would have been enough to keep the Canton and Boston merchants frantically busy. A number of the members of my family in those days must surely have worn coats and gowns lined inside for winter. Thus I may have an indirect connection with the Boston China-trade in this way as well as through porcelain.

At first, when the *Columbia* came back from China she was loaded with tea and sailed for home by way of the Cape of Good Hope. In August, 1790, she was anchored in Boston harbor after having circumnavigated the earth. Later American ships must have been loaded with china in addition to tea. Though I have been in many English homes where the ancestors had traded with China, I have never seen as much China-trade porcelain there as in and round Boston. In the big China-trade families in Boston such as the Perkinses, the Sturgises, the Cushings, the Russells, the Forbeses, the

Cunninghams, and others the china is an important heir-
loom, so I was told. The China-trade china consists of sets
of china designed and made by Chinese artists to a special
order, with American ideas incorporated in the pattern. I
cannot be sure that all the Boston China-trade china came
from Ching-te-Chen, but it is certain that it was all made
of the best china from the fine China clay, or Kaolin, and
another clay called "petuntze" out of a granite rock, *felsite*
or *petrosilex,* both of which have been available in deposit
not far from Ching-te-Chen for centuries. When I was young
I often heard of foreign orders in one big porcelain shop or
another in my hometown of Kiukiang. May I not assume
that there must be some China-trade china in Boston which
came from Kiukiang?

Nowhere can there be a better display of inimitably correct portraits of vessels of all rigs by Chinese artists than
inside the Peabody Museum of Salem. As well, there are portraits of Chinese merchants and a few descriptive landscapes
of Canton, Shanghai, Macao, and Hong Kong in the early
nineteenth century. Though they do not represent the traditional form of Chinese painting, which is seldom in oil, they
do represent that special period—the China Trade period—
when many Canton artists flourished through the patronage
of the American merchants who were not interested in traditional Chinese works but instead ordered portraits such as
those I have mentioned and one artist began to learn the
oil technique and others followed suit; they soon created
a special style of their own. At the time an Irish painter,
George Chinnery, was living in Canton and made a great
name for himself. The portrait of Houqua was painted by
Chinnery about 1852, so was the one of Chinqua. I think that
particular period of Chinese pictorial art could be called the
Chinnery period, for he actually introduced and created the

new fashion. He is said to have had a beautiful but terrifying wife, so he went to the East as an escapist. When his wife threatened to join him in Macao, he immediately departed for Canton. "Now I am all right," he said. "What a kind providence is this Chinese government that it forbids the softer sex from coming and bothering us here." The word "softer" amused me. By the Chinese imperial edict of 1757, China's foreign trade was limited to Canton, where the foreigners were restricted to the section about their rows of factories, or *hongs,* on the river front. Those who came with the foreign ships were allowed to remain in Canton only while engaged in unloading, loading, and disposing of cargoes, and then had to retire to Macao, a small island occupied and governed by the Portuguese. Not a single foreign woman would be tolerated in Canton. In 1832 Miss Harriette Low and her aunt arrived in disguise, and the Chinese immediately stopped all trade with Americans until the ladies had retreated. This must have annoyed Miss Low at the time and she must have thought the Chinese inhuman, unfriendly and most inscrutable. I am sure that many Boston women must have shed a tear with her, for they, too, were not allowed to set foot in Canton even if their shipmaster husbands consented to take them along. But what a good excuse those tall, young, handsome Yankee captains had for leaving their wives behind. The Chinese government thought that if the foreigners had no women with them they would never stay long in Canton. They did not imagine that they were providing a haven for husbands like Chinnery.

Houqua seems to have been a good, honest type of Chinese man. Probably his name, "Houqua," was not known much outside the limited commercial quarter of Canton in his lifetime or afterwards, for China then, under Confucian principles, paid very little attention to anybody who was a mere merchant busy with commercial transactions and unlearned in the Confucian classics. Houqua's real Chinese name was Wu Ping-ch'ien. His life and dealings with the Boston traders are not to be found in any Chinese annals. But from the little I have learnt of him, I feel that the part Houqua played in fostering the friendly feeling and good relations between China and America is great and should not be ignored. Thomas W. Ward of Salem wrote in 1809: "Houqua is at the head of the Hong, is very rich, sends good cargoes and (is) just in all his dealings, in short is a man of honor and veracity —has more business than any man in the Hong and secures twelve or fourteen American ships this year." Another Salem man, Bryant P. Tilden went to Canton on the ship *Canton* in 1815 and was entertained in Houqua's famous gardens, exciting on this occasion the wonder of the merchant's numerous children and grandchildren: "At first the children were a little shy, calling out: 'Fanquie! Fanquie!' on my approaching them, but when the good patriarch assured them that I was not a bad fanquie, or devil, we soon became acquainted." Fanquie is a Cantonese term originally meaning "foreign devil" but by degrees used to mean "foreigner" only. It is perhaps a pity that Houqua was not well-educated in the Chinese sense. Had he been able to write proper essays in readable Chinese, he might have left some interesting records and anecdotes about his contacts with the Western world in similar Hongs in the limited area—the river-front of Canton. They would have been immensely valuable to modern historians, Chinese and others, for I think the China-trade period marked the beginning of a great change in the Chinese economic system as well as bringing great wealth to many early American families, particularly in the area of Boston, and so contributing to the development of the tremendous American economic power of today. It is not easy to deal with the China trade and its influence in the West in general in a small space, but it is a subject too important to ignore altogether.

Though Houqua was not a classical scholar, he showed taste and refinement in following the Chinese tradition in his arrangement of furniture in his house, and his gardens also received admiration from his American friends. His enjoyment in collecting art must have influenced many of his American friends to bring back home with them Chinese *objects d'art* such as I have seen in Boston homes and museums. Houqua was remembered long after his death in 1843, and descendants of Boston China-trade families have talked to me of him with affection.

It should not be difficult to find out who was the first Boston man to land on Chinese soil if I wanted to. But it has not been easy for me to locate who was the first Chinese to come to Boston. To my surprise in the little unnamed cemetery at the corner of the Common between Tremont and Boylston Street I read the following on a tombstone:

Here lies Interr'd the body of Chow Manderien, a native of China. aged 19 yrs; whose death was occasioned on the 11th, Sept. 1798, by a fall from the mast of the ship, Mac of Boston. This stone is erected to his memory by his affectionate master John Boit, Jr.

Was he the first? I wish I knew.

Boston leads the great interest in Chinese art, literature, and thought and has no rival in the world. The British Museum of London has many fine specimens of Chinese bronzes, jades, and porcelains, particularly those in the Eumorfopolous Collection, and the Victoria and Albert Museum offers rich material on Chinese furniture, textiles, lacquer, etc. But no city in Europe has the good luck to house such important examples of early Chinese paintings as those from the Bigelow Collection in the Boston Museum of Fine Arts. It is a fact that Fenollosa and Kakuzo Okakura have done much to spread interest in Chinese art in Boston in particular and America in general through their writings and lectures. But I came to Boston too late to meet them and to attend their lectures. Mr. Kojiro Tomita, who kindly took me round his Asiatic Department in May, 1946, has done an even greater work in consolidating that interest for the past fifty years. His study of each example of Chinese painting in the Museum publication of the volume of Early Chinese paintings from T'ang to Yuan period displays much scholarly knowledge and delicate handling of the subject. He has not remained content with what was in the department from the Fenollosa and Okakura days. He has enriched the collection by acquiring many more fine examples of Chinese painting of all periods, including the works done by Ch'ing masters. His department seems to be fortunate in having funds for new acquisitions. But unfortunately there have not been many fine examples of Chinese painting offered for sale nowadays. Mr. Tomita is a gentle and polite scholar. He has told me that he has had much assistance from Mr. Tseng Hsien-Ch'i, a Chinese painter working under him in the same department, in finding good Chinese paintings. I was privileged to be the first to be shown a new acquisition, a painting by a Prince in the tenth century. I endorsed what he said about the picture. The beauty of a Chinese painting lies in the quality of the brushstrokes. The difference between a genuine one and a copy is very slight and subtle. Only those who actually know how to handle the Chinese brush and in fact practice it with their own hand will be able to distinguish the swift hand of a master from that of a copyist. Mr. Tomita knows his brushstrokes. The Asiatic

Department of the Boston Museum is rich in personnel. Apart from his special field of Japanese art, Mr. Robert Treat Paine, Assistant Curator, has made a study of porcelain and wood Chinese pillows, and has written a book which is unique. When I called on him one day this book of his had just come out, and a copy of it was inscribed for me and handed to me with a broad smile, which was reciprocated by an even broader one. I have enjoyed the kindness and friendship of the Asiatic Department since 1946, and ready help was there whenever I went in search of information.

The late Langdon Warner of the Fogg Museum of Art achieved more than any other Western student of Chinese art. He not only administered the Far Eastern department well, arranged its fine collection of Chinese art excellently, and made a special trip to Tun-huang, analyzing the frescos he collected from the caves there with amazing result, but he also trained many outstanding scholars in Chinese art who are now occupying leading positions in large museums and art galleries all over the United States. Professor Benjamin Rowland of Harvard University, a pupil of Langdon Warner, once told me that Warner had a special technique for rousing interest in Chinese art. Professor Rowland teaches Far Eastern art in Harvard now and has written a most authoritative book, *The Art and Architecture of India,* and many fine articles on Chinese art. I have also seen many of his water-colours in his own style. The Isabella Stewart Gardner Museum at Fenway Court also offers a few fine Chinese bronzes and porcelains such as cannot be found anywhere else.

Harvard University is renowned as the first American University to set up a chair of Chinese instruction. In 1877 came an appeal from Francis P. Knight of Boston for the maintenance of a chair of Chinese instruction. Largely through the help of Mr. E. B. Dew, who was for many years a commissioner in the Chinese Maritime Customs, a subscription fund of $8750 was raised. An old Chinese scholar, Ko K'un-hua, from the city of Ningpo, was appointed in 1879 to this new chair of Chinese instruction. One writer wrote the following in the Harvard Register for August, 1880:

Commencement Day in 1880 unfolded a new page in the history of the University. Among the assembled tutors, there was a veritable member of the ancient empire of China. Every reflective observer must have felt that the presence and mission of Ko K'un-hua, the instructor in Chinese, were creating a mysterious link between that old nation from which he had come and the youthful one to which we belong.

From this early start Harvard-Yenching Institute, established in 1921, took the lead in Chinese studies in all the states of America. They have made great contributions to the study of Chinese history, literature and thought and are now working on a special project on Chinese economic studies. Besides, Dr. A. K'aiming Ch'iu told me that he was asked to come to organise the Chinese-Japanese Library at Harvard in 1927 and has been on the job ever since. His name is connected with the first few in this special field, and the Chinese-Japanese Library ranks next only to the Oriental Department of the Library of Congress. China is much alive in Boston and its neighbourhood.

Professor L. S. Yang, Professor of Chinese language, with whom I stayed for a while in his house in Cambridge, once showed a photograph of the first instructor, Ko K'un-hua, and told me an anecdote about him. Ko had brought a servant with him to Harvard. The College authorities had allotted the second floor of a building in Harvard Yard to

Ko, and Ko's servant was put in the attic of the same building. As soon as Ko learned this he insisted on moving up to live in the attic and let his servant occupy the second floor. His reason was that no servant could possibly occupy a position above his master. I said to Yang: "I suppose this is according to one of Confucius's principles." We both laughed. I then asked Yang if he had thought of bringing a servant with him to teach at Harvard?

"We wish MIT could do some research to unify our colors, sizes, and heights."

XIV

Boston Brother

I LOOK on Boston and Cambridge as brothers, as far as literary and academic twins in their literary circles are concerned. I have read that between 1630 and 1647 about one hundred University men had come from England to the Massachusetts Bay Colony. Most of them settled within five miles of Boston or Cambridge. Though many of them were clerics, the rest represented various professions, so in Boston and Cambridge society was learned and cultivated from the very beginning. It is no wonder that nowadays there are so many higher educational institutions in Boston, Cambridge, and the neighbourhood. Among all of them, Harvard College in Cambridge is the oldest in the whole United States.

Strangely enough, I came from England in 1952 with the intention of seeing Boston, but I became acquainted with Cambridge first, as my friend, Yang Lien-sheng, Professor of Chinese, lives there. I used to follow him through Harvard Yard, getting to know one building after the other. The buildings confused my eyes somewhat in the beginning, for I had been so long used to the yellowish, mellow stone of Oxford University. Gradually each one revealed to me its individual character and its place in the whole. The trees of Harvard Yard bring the buildings into harmony with one another, they break the straight lines and they prevent the eye from making comparisons between one building and another. The colors of the tree leaves in the different seasons tint the walls, and the trees in full leaf alter the shapes of the buildings. In winter the dark trunks and branches of the trees form intriguing interlaced patterns in the center of the Yard, while the red brick of the building sprays a reddish hue over the white snow on the ground. Harvard Yard with its trees has made Harvard University. The term "University campus" in all other American universities must have been a later invention. Harvard was wise not to have quadrangles like those in Oxford Colleges, with their fresh green lawns. Harvard is a university marching with the times, as its various buildings show.

Being no student of architecture I found the clean white spire of the University Chapel facing the splendid façade of the Widener Memorial Library, with its Corinthian columns and broad flight of granite steps, an unusually pleasant balance of elegance and grandeur. One might expect a long stretch of wide open ground in front of the Widener Library to enhance its majestic bearing, but the trees in the Yard suggest depth instead. Without the trees the University Chapel might look too exposed and too genteel in comparison with the strong colonnade of mighty stone pillars of the Widener Library. As it is, the two buildings exchange smiles over the tree-tops and through the holes between the leaves.

Most of the trees are American elms, tall and full of strength. But one pine tree on the chapel side appeals to me especially. There is a smaller one near Boylston Hall. Pines have been a favourite subject for the Chinese artist since the tenth century. They have a distinctive character and stand out among all trees. They grow abundantly in the Chinese countryside and on the hills. Even in the most rocky parts of the mountainous region of China, where little soil remains and where no other tree can grow, they flourish.

Their strong-built, twisted trunks and branches suggest
naturalness and aesthetic forms. They suit Chinese brush-
work and fit into Chinese artistic composition admirably.
With their bluish-green needles and scaly, ochre-coloured
bark, they are very decorative in a landscape garden and are
always included as an important item in the art of Chinese
garden design. Confucius in the fifth century B.C. said:
"Only when the year turns cold can we see that the pines
and cypresses are the last to fade." Chuang Tzu in the third
century B.C. recognized the vigor of the pines and cypresses
in time of frost and snow. Again, Chuang Tzu remarked:
"Were it not for cold weather we would not know the
character of the pines and cypresses; if things were not
difficult we could hardly find the gentleman." From these
sayings the pines became in the Chinese mind a symbol of
a gentleman with a very strong character and a symbol of
long life. In Harvard Yard the three pines suggest to me
that the great institution of learning will live for ever, and
that its scholars will continue to be of strong character.

I was told that Widener Library houses some five million
books. It may be the largest university library in the United
States, if not in the whole world. I do not know. I saw the
Sargent mural paintings on the staircases after I had read
of the controversy caused by them among Harvard students
at the time they were put up. The mural paintings are a
symbolic representation of the part American youth played
in the First World War. Technically speaking, Sargent
splashed on his pigments with his inimitable craftsmanship
as in his other works in the Boston Public Library, the
Boston Museum of Fine Arts, and the Gardner Museum at
Fenway Court. He was acclaimed as the greatest living artist
at the time. In those days any work he produced caused great
enthusiasm among the circles in which he was known. I have

no doubt about the genuineness of the enthusiasm, but I am inclined to think that fashion played a part in it. This is only natural. Well-known artists of today have their following too. It is after the death of the artist that his work is objectively and genuinely judged. Sargent's name will live, but to my mind not all the works he produced will enjoy everlasting fame. This may be true of many great artists. Many attribute the dispute about these murals to the change in artistic taste and to the new trend in the appreciation of the art of today. But I think the modern trend in art appreciation is the result of the change of our mind towards things as a whole. Art was first in the service of religion; then it was in the hands of kings and nobles; later it glorified heroic deeds and the achievement of fame and wealth; and now it serves to express the complications of human consciousness and subconsciousness. The glorification of heroic deeds was a passing phase. The petition sent in by a number of Harvard students for the removal of the mural paintings from Widener was caused by their subject matter and was not aimed against the artist himself. Those who want to adorn the walls of many modernistic edifices with modern art should take note. Indeed, to achieve an important architectural design for a big building is extremely difficult, but the interior decoration is perhaps more difficult still if it is meant to be lasting. Do we try to aim at lasting value nowadays?

The well-proportioned building with the mellow ivy-covered front is University Hall, situated almost in the center of the Yard facing the main gateway. Not long after my arrival in Cambridge a Boston photographer was sent to take a photograph of Professor Yang and me for reproduction in a magazine called *The World,* published by the Information Service of the State Department in Washington.

Two photographs were taken, one on the steps of Widener Library and the other in front of University Hall, close to the bronze statue of John Harvard. After the photographer had left us, Yang pointed out the words on the pedestal of the statue, "John Harvard, Founder, 1638."

Harvard: "They even have doubts of me."

A friend once told me that it is generally known as the "Statue of the three Lies." One is that Harvard was founded in 1636, not 1638. The second, that John Harvard had nothing to do with Harvard. And the third, that the statue represented an imaginary person, not John Harvard himself, for no one knew what he had looked like. I felt puzzled. I thought the inscription was unusual. It did not give the dates of birth and death after the word "Founder." If the sculptor, Daniel Chester French, had inserted the letter "d." before 1638, one possible lie would have been removed. It is a known fact that John Harvard did bequeath his books and fortune to the College. Professor Samuel Morison wrote: "The collection (of books) does credit to John Harvard's catholic learning and good taste. . . . That such a collection could be brought out to a country only seven years settled is striking evidence of the Puritan purpose to maintain intellectual standards in the New World." So it cannot be said that John Harvard had nothing to do with Harvard. The word "Founder" is perhaps a mistake. Regarding the likeness of the statue, when did Daniel French execute this work? The main point is how and why the name of Harvard was chosen for the College. I was interested to read the following passage from the Secretary of the Harvard Club of London:

> The 350th anniversary of the baptism of John Harvard in Southwark Cathedral will be commemorated in a special service to be held in the Cathedral Friday, November 29, at 5.15. The Provost and the Precentor will officiate, and the Lord Bishop of Southwark will give the address.
> It is hoped that many Harvard men, their families, and friends will be able to attend.

After all, Harvard men have accepted John Harvard, so why need anyone else worry? I said to my friend that we Chinese believe that Westerners always have records in minute detail going back for centuries, yet here was a record missing. How could we ourselves hope to know of events and persons in the Han or T'ang dynasties hundreds of years ago? He gave me an uncompromising smile.

I have another personal association with University Hall. David McCord asked me if I would like to do a design of Harvard Yard for the Harvard Fund blotter. We roamed the Yard for a while and I then chose University Hall for my composition. When I finished the work David and his friends were a little uneasy about the bright-red ivy. Ivy, they said, is always green. I made it red, remembering the red creeper on the walls of many Oxford colleges in England in September and thinking the mellow University Hall would be enhanced by some Indian Summer colouring. Strangely enough, the people of New England admire the Indian Summer colouring in the countryside of Connecticut, Vermont, and New Hampshire, but tend to forget about colour near at home.

One building has light yellow walls instead of red brick. That is Wadsworth house, built in 1726, and formerly the home of Harvard presidents. David McCord, as the Secretary of the Harvard Fund Council, has his office there. Since our friendship began, I have visited him in his office after office hours whenever I was in Cambridge. I was told that through the door by which I went in and out Ralph Waldo Emerson used to do likewise when he was "President's messenger," working his way through Harvard. Not that I am in any way comparable to that great man, but some strangely exact coincidences in our lives embolden me to mention my name with his. Emerson was born in 1803; I, in 1903. Emerson set foot in England for the first time in 1833; I reached London from China in 1933. At that point we diverge. Emerson did not stay long in England; he did not need to learn the language, and he saw little in England that he could not see in his own America. I remained in England for over twenty years, with occasional visits to America and other countries. Yet here at Harvard I was popping in and out of Wadsworth house, like him, but not so fortunate as to be able to work my way through Harvard by doing so. From the windows of David's office he sees birds, chipmunks, squirrels, and the five big beech trees in Harvard Yard. He often suggested that we step out for a close look at his trees. He has many theories about them. Each one, and even each single branch, means something to him. I endorse his words on the beautiful shapes of two of the beeches. Through David I can see how much Harvard men love Harvard Yard and the trees in it.

Talking about trees in Harvard Yard, I could not help expressing my great amazement at the unusual collection of flowers and plants in the Agassiz Museum. I bought the pamphlet showing a colour photograph of a flowering twig and many black-and-white photographs of other plants. When I was informed that they were all made of glass, I could not believe my eyes, for I had taken them to be photographs of real plants. But to my great amazement many flowers and many plants, shown in the cases, were all made of glass even to the tiny, hair-like stamens and pistils. It did not seem possible, yet there they were. I was amazed at the ingenuity of the human fingers and brain. I may have used the word *finger* wrongly. I spent five years in learning chemistry and did learn how to blow some small, thin glass tubes, but I could never have touched the glass by hand, for it was far too hot. I should probably not judge by my own limited experience.

The old attendant of the Agassiz, who must have looked after the glass flowers for years, walked slowly towards me and whispered and sighed to me that the glass flowers were far too delicate and that many of them had lost something or were broken beyond repair. There was no one in the world able to repair them, for the making of them was a completely lost art. He added that the museum floor was not specially made for such delicate displays. The heavy stamp of a foot from a visitor would cause vibration of the stamens or pistils of the tiny flowers inside the case, though no such motion could be detected by any human eye.

I then learned how the collection of the glass flowers was formed and came to Harvard. It was an idea of Professor Goodale's, who went in 1886 to see Leopold Blaschka in Dresden, Germany, for some glass models of plants for his Botany class. Blaschka, famous for his dexterity in patterning

Ducks in Jamaica Pond

Pine in Harvard Yard

glass to the most intricate models, was a Bohemian artist and had no interest in money. He rejected the request flatly, saying that he knew nothing of Botany. While leaving the premises Professor Goodale exclaimed at the beauty of a small cluster of little butterfly orchids. Blaschka laughed and said that the orchids were made of glass. Immediately he was caught and promised to make the experiment. Then his son, Rudolph Blaschka, came to study at Harvard and took back many plants of the desert and of tropical America for his father and himself to work at. By and by, through their diligent labor, thousands of models of flowers were shipped to Harvard. The way they packed the glass models in boxes was said to be most ingenious too. In 1895, Rudolph Blaschka came again to make a collection of flowers in Virginia but was suddenly called back to his father's death-bed. The son then worked on alone on the models. Old Blaschka had not wanted to train any apprentice or assistant but his son. Nor did Rudolph. Unfortunately Rudolph had no son, so the art died with him. It is a pity. This kind of unique craftsman was not uncommon in China. We have many stories about some wonderful jade-carver who could work out most intricate patterns by making use of different colours in a raw piece of jade or some clever ivory-engraver who could engrave the finest designs on ten or twelve balls, one inside the other in sequence without a hinge, at the end of an elephant's tusk. None of them wanted any apprentice and their art died with them. Indeed, Chinese craftsmanship through all forms of Chinese art—in bronze, jade, ceramics, ivory, lacquer, wood, and stone—is very well known throughout the world. Yet glass has never been a good workable medium for Chinese artists, though we have produced some fine glassware. China had not produced a Blaschka. But I think the ingenious brain of some Chinese craftsman could have helped them to work out models in porcelain, ivory, or wood on as fine a scale as Blaschka did in glass. Unfortunately we had no botanist like Professor Goodale. Names of Chinese artists and craftsmen seldom went far beyond their birthplace.

Only recently I paid a visit to the Chicago Natural History Museum and was most intrigued by their botanical exhibits, as fascinating as the Blaschka glass flowers. All the exhibits are life-size and many could easily be mistaken for real plants brought from some jungle in South America. The finest stamens and pistils of the tiniest flowers are all there, too. This immediately made me realise that, though the Blaschka art had died with the father and son, a similar art has grown up in Chicago. I wanted to meet the artists and learn something about their method, but lack of time made it impossible. Fortunately Dr. Kenneth Starr, Curator of the Department of Chinese art and crafts, could give me a brief idea of the manner in which the reproductions are made.

A variety of materials is used. The stems and woody parts are generally made of wax, over an iron wire frame. Wax also is used for the large fruits (hollow-cast) and large leaves. Plastics of various kinds (cellulose, tenite) are used for leaves, small berries, petals of blossoms, etc. Plaster also is used, though only for the *very* large fruits, which are hollow-cast in plaster. Glass is used for the most delicate parts, such as the stamens and pistils for the blossoms, and such things as small berries, etc. This last point interested me enormously, for, I thought, Blaschka's art did not die out. Someone must have come to study his products in the Agassiz and have worked out ways of imitating his method as he imitated Nature. I felt myself fortunate to have seen the glass flowers in Agassiz and the botanical exhibits in Chicago.

Also they make me think how much more fortunate

young students of today are to have such fine botanical specimens for their studies. Indeed, American youngsters of today are far more fortunate than their brothers and sisters in many other parts of the world. Should they not do much better work with so many advantages? At the same time, I have reflected that no matter how ingenious the human brain be, Blaschka, his son, and many others are mere copyists, not creators. The real artist is still Nature. We Chinese and perhaps many Orientals have the notion that Western civilization aims at overcoming Nature or conquering Nature. But as far as productivity and resourcefulness are concerned, man's effort is negligible in comparison with Nature's. For instance, Nature has made use of all kinds of colours to produce countless varieties of flowers and birds' plumage, none of which is too unpleasant and too disagreeable to human eyes. What have we men produced with the same colours? Man has always been bothered by the mystery of Nature's power. Man feared Nature at first, then inquired about her, then studied her and imitated her and is still doing so. There is still endless mystery about Nature. Why did Nature produce such startlingly beautiful plumage for the peacock, yet give it such a voice? Why did Nature create the pig with such a stupid face although it is far from being a stupid animal? There will not be an answer to these questions in my lifetime.

The best place for the study of man himself, I was told, is the Peabody Museum along Divinity Avenue. I paid it a visit, not to find out about my most remote ancestors, but because I was greatly attracted by the number of exhibits—Mayan, Aztec, Mexican, etc. I have always maintained a belief that our forefathers in China had a lot to do with those of the American Indians in the very remote days. The designs on the head-dresses of some exhibits bear striking resemblances to those on some Shang and early Chou bronzes. Though no systematic study of the relation between ancient China and ancient America has yet been made, many people have begun to touch on one subject or another. In the recent publication of the Peabody Museum of Archaeology and Ethnology, *A Study of Navajo Symbolism,* Miss Mary C. Wheelwright wrote "Notes on Corresponding Symbols in Various Parts of the World," in which she discussed many points of similarity between the Navajo mind and that of some of the Chinese. She says that in Navajo sand-paintings the Sun, Moon, Earth-Mother, Sky-Father, and storms are always represented with horns of power. In her opinion, horned animals in the form of a bull, antlered deer, or antelope, were considered one of the earliest sources of power in all ancient races. This interests me greatly, for I think it may offer one of the better explanations of the principal animal motif of the early bronze art of the Shang dynasty of the 16th century B.C. The motif is a design or pattern, called *t'ao t'ieh* in Chinese, of an ogre-like head of a horned animal with massive muzzle and huge staring eyes. It appears on almost every one of the Chinese early bronzes and other antique objects. It is obvious that it played an important part in the mythology of the early Chinese. Yet no one, either Chinese or Western scholar, has found any definite idea behind it. Many just call it Monster mask or ogre mask. No ancient literature about it has yet come to light. The Chinese name, *t'ao t'ieh,* was given by some scholar-connoisseur of the Sung dynasty (960–1279). The surface meaning of the two Chinese words put together is "a gluttonous creature," which seems to be most appropriate, as the bronze vessels were chiefly used as food or wine containers. The design of *t'ao t'ieh,* though varying from one bronze vessel to another, is invariably an animal head with

horns. It could be there in such a persistent manner simply
to denote the ancient belief in power in the mind of the
early Chinese. I suppose in the most remote days when
man had not yet discovered ways and means of hunting or
of protecting himself, his thought turned to the horned
animals such as bulls, stags, or goats, which were so well-
equipped for defense. Lions were never found in China.
Tigers were not familiar to man. Therefore the early Chinese
imagination went as far as it could in designing *t'ao t'ieh* in
the most uncompromising manner possible. This may also
explain the Chinese idea of "dragon," which is a most
fabulous imaginary powerful but benevolent animal, always
with horns, symbolising the imperial ruler from very ancient
times.

Cambridge caused me embarrassment more than once.
The most embarrassing moment I had there was at the
Harvard–Yale Football Match of 1953. Arthur Walworth
got a ticket for me. Three days before the match Mr. John
Nichols wrote to tell me to be sure in Boston to meet his
son, Captain of the Harvard team, in the Harvard Club.
We met and shook hands heartily. Mr. John Nichols Jr.
is not different from any other young American—strongly
built as a captain of a football team should be. I promised
them both to be there to see the match, for sure. The date
of the match arrived. It was a grey, English type of day
—cold and snowing a little at first. Only a few Radcliffe
girls, presumably, wearing striking red-and-yellow jumpers,
made bright spots here and there under the overcast sky.
The throng became denser each step on our way to the
Harvard Stadium. I soon found my seat between Arthur
Walworth and his friend. In no time all the seats were
filled. Bugles blew and a band played. One or two clownlike

creatures ran east and ran west, raising their hands up and
down, while a number of tuxedoed young men sang as loudly
as they could along the bottom of the rows of benches directly
opposite to us. But the wind was blowing away from us and
I could not hear a word of the song. Then a bunch of young
men in white with red stripes came to the center of the
ground and walked into several patterns, one of which was
the year, 1953. All this was new from my knowledge of
English football matches, particularly the one between
Oxford and Cambridge, and I wondered how many took
part in the game. Soon a few more in the same kind of
uniform came to replace the first lot. I craned my neck
to see if I could recognise the sturdy Captain of the Harvard
team. There seemed a big darkish blur in the center. I was
lent a pair of field-glasses. I saw no Mr. Nichols, Jr., but
instead a tallish young fellow with very prominent square
shoulders looking exactly like the marble life-size statue of
King Mycerinus from the Mycerinus Pyramid Temple at
Giza, Dynasty IV, ca. 2595–2570 B.C., which I had seen in
the Boston Museum of Fine Arts. The rest of the team were
all Egyptians, I thought. While I was still craning, Arthur
and his friend suddenly jumped on the seats and clapped
their hands madly. So did everybody else. A moment later
they repeated their jump and shouted "Oh." This performance was repeated again and again. I did not know
what it was about, though by now I was jumping up and
sitting down too. And when my friend laughed, I could
not help laughing, like the blind man in the following
Chinese joke:

A party of men sat together talking. One of them was
blind. Suddenly something they saw struck them as laughable
and they laughed. The blind man laughed too. The rest of

the party looked at him in surprise and asked: "What did you see that made you laugh?" The answer was: "Friends, you were of course laughing at something laughable: surely you wouldn't play a trick on me."

Oxford human giraffe and Harvard modern Mycerinus

So I trusted my friend completely and waited on patiently for the game to begin. Eventually impatience did get hold of me and I asked: "When will the game begin?" My question coincided with another jump and a roar of laughter at something happening in the center of the ground; then Arthur said "The game is nearly half over—this is American football, not English Rugby!" I sat down and felt downcast, saying to myself: "So far I have not seen the ball kicked once. They are playing with their hands and shoulders, not their feet. They should call the game *handball*, not *football*. Well, this is America, not England." I kept quiet. I knew that I had been a fool, and did not want to make matters worse by asking any more questions. In fact I am no sportsman and know very little about football or "handball" games. I had come to watch the match in order to keep my promise to Mr. Nichols and his Captain son.

More shouting and laughter occurred. And more jumping-up-and-sitting-down among those around me. I thought I was in the Monkey House of the Bronx Zoo, New York,

Football or handball?

watching the Capuchin monkeys moving their bodies up and down incessantly on the bars, waiting for the keeper to bring their share of fruit. Another loud roar of laughter arose. The commotion around me increased. Many people did not sit down again but started to move away from their seats. Some even stood on the seats, throwing their caps in the air and shouting and singing, but no tune that I knew. The game was over. I whispered to my friend: which side won? "Yale, of course. I am a Yale man" was the excited answer. This proved much too much for me. I had been sitting on the wrong side of the game, the Yale side. So without uttering a word, I tried to get away. Unfortunately my right hand was seized by my friend, who dragged me with him to see the last act of the ceremonious rites of the American "football" game. It was a race to the goalposts to pull them down and smash them ruthlessly. All were struggling to get hold of a small piece of a post. I was told that the piece, if one managed to get one, would be placed in an honored position in the owner's house as a most treasured souvenir. Do both teams' supporters try to get a piece of wood? I asked. "Chiefly the winner's side, of course." This "of course" made me loosen my hand from my friend's and I then made the excuse that I must get back to my place in Pinckney Street up Beacon Hill. I had planned to find Mr. Nichols and to shake hands again with his Captain son after the game, but I did not dare to, now. I felt most uncomfortable. I thought, though they speak almost exactly the same language, the Americans do things quite differently from the English in many respects. The game of football must have come from England at first, but gradually the Americans have evolved new rules until it is a different game. People in the West tend to think that the Chinese always do things the other way round to theirs. Now I have learnt that the Americans play football with their hands. What does it matter, after all? No two individuals do things in exactly the same manner. Nevertheless, I know that I should have managed to sit on the Harvard side on that Harvard–Yale Match day.

Early in my stay in Boston I was told that one could always tell a Harvard man—but one just could not tell him much. After a few months' stay in Boston and Cambridge, I found out the truth of the second half of the saying. But I cannot always tell a Harvard man! Perhaps it was much easier in the early days, for people in different walks of life then did dress differently. The English did, so did the Chinese, and the early Americans did too. I do not refer to the different tribes of the American Indians. When I looked at etchings and photographs of Harvard men of the past, I found Puritan Harvard men like the statue of John Harvard in the Yard, Georgian-English Harvard men, Victorian-English Harvard men and bowler-hatted-English Harvard men of only forty years ago. I was most amused to find, when I turned over the photographs of the football-match spectators from 1900 to 1914, that nearly every man wore a black bowler hat like the English. No doubt most of them were Harvard men of the time. In London before the Second World War I saw the bankers and stockbrokers of the City wearing bowlers, but did not notice many bowlers elsewhere. During the war not one was to be seen. After the war bowlers gradually made a small comeback. However, a bowler hat definitely signifies an Englishman and no other. I do not know what England looked like before 1933. But when I reached England then, the English type of suit and hat was the most fashionable in the world. It is no wonder that most of the spectators at the football matches between Harvard and Yale used to like to wear bowlers. But I cannot conclude that they were Harvard men. They may just as easily have been Yale men. And now neither Harvard nor Yale men bother much about headgear.

An Oxford man is just as hard for me to tell as a Harvard man. But I became artful while living in Oxford. I used to bring the word "Cambridge" casually into the conversation when talking to a new acquaintance who might have belonged to either University. It always called forth some remark, which told me all I wanted to know. I used the same dodge with the word Yale in Boston and New York, trying to isolate Harvard men, but without success. I was just as

likely to hear about Columbia, Princeton, Michigan or
Chicago. My other dodge, to talk about fathers and grand-
fathers, had better results. This dodge certainly would not
work in Oxford today, for most of my English friends, if
they had two sons, would tell me that they hoped one son
would go to Oxford and the other to Cambridge. So a
Cambridge man might have an Oxford-man grandfather and
vice versa. But a Harvard-man grandfather would have a
Harvard-man son and a Harvard-man grandson and so on.
Not only that, he would have a Radcliffe-girl granddaughter,
too.

Whilst I was enjoying experimenting with my dodge one
of my Chinese friends said superciliously that I was busying
myself with nothing. I think life is after all full of "nothing"
business. One's capability of busying oneself with nothing-
ness can be a measure of one's capacity to enjoy life.

An Oxford undergraduate or postgraduate can be detected
by his pipe, his colourful long woolly scarf wound round his
neck in many rings, making him like a human giraffe, and
his corduroy trousers. A freshman always wears a short jacket-
like black gown. A Harvard undergraduate may smoke a pipe
or wear corduroy trousers, but he seldom has a woolly scarf
round his neck, and never a long one, and does not put up
with any gown at all. I entered the Lamont Library several
times in order to find a clue to the Harvard man. The library
revealed itself as a paradise for an artist, for there were all
kinds of unimaginable and unthinkable poses to be sketched.
I have not been in Cambridge long enough yet. The activities
of the undergraduates inside the dormitories are still unknown to me, but I have often heard the sound of gramophone records drifting through the windows when I happened to be passing through Harvard Yard. The Harvard
Band seems to practice more energetically in spring than in

winter. What I have missed nostalgically is the type of debate which takes place in the Oxford Student Union during term.

Perhaps one thing is typical of Harvard which I have not seen anywhere else; that is, the green cloth bag for books. Not every Harvard undergraduate carries a green cloth bag, but quite a few do. There seem to be a number of ways of carrying it, and I have made some sketches of them. It puz-

zles me why Harvard students usually have to carry books about. I do not remember seeing Oxford students doing the same. Do Harvard students spend more of their time on books than their Oxford counterparts? Oxford students have their afternoons taken up with parties, chiefly tea parties, which most of the Harvard students have probably not heard of, except the Boston Tea Party.

Dr. Elliott Perkins, Master of Lowell House, and Dr. Walter Whitehill, formerly Senior Tutor of the same house—each has his individual way of carrying the green cloth bag. Dr. Whitehill holds the bag by the top in his right hand, while in his left he carries a pipe which moves up and down slowly in time with his walking gait in the manner of Sir John Falstaff in a Shakespeare play. Dr. Perkins throws the bag over his right shoulder, holds the string in his right hand, and walks along firmly, looking straight ahead and pressing his lips together tightly. Through the kindness of both men I was able to sample a feast at the high table of Lowell House. The dinner was given in honour of Sir Herbert Read, who had come to deliver the Norton Lectures for the semester. Lowell House is the only college to have the high-table system in all the United States. It was originated by Julian L. Coolidge when he was the first Master of Lowell House. He was an Oxford man and liked the high-table idea very much. In Oxford the custom is that all the students of the College sitting at the lower tables stand up when the Master comes in, followed by his guests, professors, and tutors. Before sitting down the Master says a prayer in Latin. This was not the case in Lowell House. After Dr. Perkins had led Sir Herbert Read and the rest of us to the high table, it soon became a happy chattering hall and everyone ate with gusto. I was placed between two young Harvard men who were to receive their Ph.D. degrees in a few months' time. Both were delightful fellows and had much to tell each other as well as me. I do not know how our talk came to dating, a subject on which I have still a great deal to learn. Both my neighbours had great theories. One had worked out a system for dating according to a slight difference in age, to the time of the day and the week, as well as to the distance of the meeting-place from the damsel's home. The other said that he had not had a single day without a date since coming to Harvard. Many days he had had two or three dates. I remarked that timing must need to be very accurate and must be his constant worry. I also thought that a very small alarm-clock which could be worn behind the ear like a

hearing-aid would be useful. Fortunately most Harvard students have cars of their own and can get about quickly. My
second neighbour expressed his preference for Wellesley
College, finding Radcliffe too close at hand and leading to
too much gossip. After listening to all this I realised that
Harvard students did have as much leisure as their Oxford
brothers. The English educational system puts great stress
on the secondary-school years. There was once a cartoon in

Punch: It showed three persons—one young man about
seventeen working diligently at a desk while his father was
receiving a friend who had just dropped in. Having noticed
how hard the young man was working, the guest remarked
to him: "Don't work so hard." But the father retorted:
"Never mind. He will have three years' holiday at Oxford."
No doubt all the Harvard undergraduates are having their
holiday in Harvard.

At no time had I seen more Harvard men, old and young,
sitting together than I experienced on Commencement Day,
held in the Tercentenary Theatre at Cambridge, June 11,
1953. Professor Yang selected the seats and got the tickets
for his family and me. I was to look after the family while

he joined the academic procession in the ceremony. Mrs. Yang, her daughter, Lili Shu-li, her son, Tommy Te-Cheng, and I reached our seats in very good time. Many seats were still unoccupied. We watched others, particularly the ladies in bright-coloured dresses, streaming in from all sides. This was a happy day for Harvard men and their families, relations, and friends. The whole space of the Yard was soon

filled and our eyes could not reach far beyond the people sitting in the next two or three rows. A moment before, my eyes had been circling round on eye-level, but now I looked up over the heads of my fellow-guests. It was a bright sunny day, warm but not too hot. There was a gentle breeze tiptoeing in and out among all the heads. I watched the leaves of the elms turning clockwise and then anti-clockwise as if some invisible hand were causing them to dance for the occasion and join in the enjoyment. Not one face looked solemn. I had often seen the graduation ceremony in the Sheldonian Theatre in Oxford University. This was the first time I had been present at Harvard Commencement. From where I was sitting, I could not see what was going on. A

stream of moving heads appeared in the center, and gradually
figures in long gowns climbed up the platform and took
their seats. The strains of the Commencement hymn sung
by the University Choir in crimson gowns came over the
air from the steps of University Hall. I could see the upper
back view of the conductor raising his arms and moving
them vigorously while the sleeves of his gown flapped in the

air. I made a quick rough sketch in pencil. All of a sudden,
out of the blue came a cheerful blast of thunder—*"Saluto!*
Saluto!! Saluto!!!" from the platform. Nathan Alfred Haver-
stock was speaking his Latin Salutatory Disquisition. *De*
Rebus Futuris, to us. Not a word except *Saluto* was clear
to me, but the speaker's happy voice, broad smile, wide-
stretched arms and manner of tilting his body backwards
and swinging then in a semicircle made the salutation most
effective. After Roger Allan Moore's English Disquisition
on Congress, Socrates, and Harvard, President James Bryant
Conant bestowed the various degrees to those presented by
their deans, masters, and principals and the honorary doctor's

degrees. Finally most of the spectators and many taking part in the ceremony sampled the excellent ham-and-turkey-sandwich luncheon with great enjoyment in another part of Harvard Yard. Oxford could never afford to entertain so many guests. While eating, a number of people in top hats and tails, black as well as grey, each with a short black rod in his hand, moved round the Yard and talked in groups.

They reminded me of groups I had seen at the Derby in England. They were Overseers, an important body of the University. The rod was the symbol of their authority.

Many unexpected experiences befell me after I came to give a course on the general outline of Chinese Culture at Columbia University, New York, in September, 1955. One of them was an invitation to deliver the Phi Beta Kappa Oration at Harvard University on 11 June, 1956, a day before the Commencement Exercises of that year. It was the greatest honour that was ever bestowed on me, yet I was bewildered at the moment of receiving the invitation. I did not know how to handle the situation for a while. It was suggested to me that I should speak on the Chinese scholar, and I could not but agree that it would be a subject wonderfully suitable to the tradition of the occasion, for the great Emerson had previously delivered his famous oration on "The American Scholar." But after serious thought I realised that it would have to be on the Chinese Painter that I should speak. Reasons for this choice were many. The chief one was that the subject "The Chinese Scholar" would cover a wide range and could not be summarised in a concise study, particularly as the original meaning of the word *shih*, or "scholar," in Chinese is obscure and even ambiguous, though of great antiquity. On the other hand, I found only four times the word "American" in the whole long oration that Emerson delivered. Leaving those four words out, his oration on the Man-thinking man or "scholar" was to the world at large. His "self-reliance" principle was not only for American scholars but for all throughout the world; not only for his contemporaries but for all generations. It was unfortunate that in his time Emerson had to make a specific announcement; thus his oration became known as the American "intellectual Declaration of Independence." This is unavoidably misleading, I think. We modern men are the products of the crossing of cultures, and it does not become us to make much of our differences. Beneath the schools and techniques lies the poetic truth of Man and of Nature, the basis of all civilisation. It is civilisation, rather than national culture, for which recognition is needed.

Dr. Elliott Perkins was kind enough to ask me to spend the night before the Oration in the rooms which are generally assigned to guests and ministers in Lowell House. I had a very comfortable night. Having put on Chinese national costume, I was fetched by Walter Whitehill in his crimson gown of London University. He is the chief marshall of the Harvard Chapter of Phi Beta Kappa. We then met Dr. Perkins in his black Harvard gown near the entrance of the house, and walked over to Harvard Yard, where many gowned professors and deans stood waiting near University Hall. Then came President Nathan Marsh Pusey. After much greeting, a fife-and-drum corps led the procession to the Sanders Theatre of the great Memorial Hall. Behind the drummers walked the Chief Marshall, then the President of the University, the President of the Harvard Chapter of Phi Beta Kappa, the Master of Lowell House, and the Dean of the Graduate School. Professor John Holmes of Tufts University and I walked side by side and a number of professors followed. After the opening prayer and the presidential address by Van Wyck Brooks, Professor Holmes read his beautiful long poem before my oration. Afterwards we attended the luncheon party given by the Harvard Chapter at Fogg Museum, where eight newly elected members were given a citation and a certificate. My oration was recorded by the Boston Broadcast Corporation and was broadcast in the evening. I was told that I was only the second Oriental to have been asked to deliver an oration for the Phi Beta Kappa, the first being Rabindranath Tagore. This made me feel even more overwhelmed by the honour. It was a memorable day for me.

I had been asked to take part in the Procession on Commencement Day, so I remained in Lowell House for two more nights. A Piper in Scottish tartan woke all of us up with his piping at six-thirty as before. In the dining hall Dr. Perkins made a moving farewell speech to those who would leave Lowell House after Commencement Day. Then we moved together to Harvard Yard. When we were crossing Massachusetts Avenue three policemen brought the traffic to a standstill on our behalf. In the Yard we waited in front of Massachusetts Hall for the arrival of the Governor of Massachusetts and the Sheriff of Middlesex County. Many people who had crowded inside the main gateway were told to step back by the police, when a few scarlet-coated lancers with banners and spears trotted in to make way for the Governor. These lancers on horseback, I was told, were the successors to the eight pikemen who served at the first Harvard Commencement in 1642. After Governor Herter had been greeted by President Pusey and others, Dr. Perkins mounted a tall structure to announce the names of each group—the President, the Governor, the overseers, recipients of the honorary degrees, the deans and masters, the academic professors, and so on, who moved by in order. My name came after the group of the Harvard Class of 1896. Walter Whitehill was walking beside me as escort. We moved very slowly and passed through the channel in the center of the Yard in front of the Widener Library, the part of the proceedings which I had not been able to see very well in 1953. Walter and I followed the Class of 1896 up to the platform and sat a little way to the right of the President. The uniformed Sheriff of Middlesex County stepped forward on the platform and struck it three times with his old-fashioned sword, calling the meeting to order. I could now see the crowd in front of the platform as a whole but was unable to gaze at things in detail. The temperature was above one hundred degrees Fahrenheit. An extraordinarily strong wind the night before had blown the canopy which covered the platform into shreds and it had not been possible to replace it in time. So the President and the rest of us on the platform were exposed to a hotter sun than I ever experienced in England in more than twenty years. They were all in their heavy gowns and academic caps. I could take my hat off and wipe my face now and then, but some did not seem to be able to do that. Or they were not prepared to do so. I was ready for any emergency, for several elderly gentlemen, each looking over eighty, were sitting not far from where I was and they all had heavy suits on, too. Two of them just could not open their eyes, nor keep their mouths shut, and the slender chairs did not seem to support their bodies sufficiently. Fortunately someone brought out ice-water and gave us each a cup of it from time to time. We

A family gathering at Lowell House

all survived. Nothing made us happier than to step off that platform at the end of the proceedings. I was told that Harvard Commencement Exercises are America's oldest spectacle. They have gone on for the past three hundred years. They will no doubt go on for another three hundred years if not for ever. Will modern development in art, music, and literature begin to play a part in this traditional spectacle in future?

There are many fine places for walking in Cambridge. The long Brattle Street is one. Along it there are many fine old houses including Longfellow House and Elmwood

House. Dr. Denman Ross used to say that no gentleman in Cambridge walked, except upon Brattle Street, unless he had business elsewhere. It was also along Brattle Street that Professor James Russell Lowell used to dash to his class in dressing-gown, slippers, and cap. Longfellow was often seen on Brattle Street taking his morning and evening stroll, sometimes accompanied by his dear wife and later by his friend Emerson, and others. There must have been people, particularly women, who came to walk there, just to get a glimpse of the poet or to make a personal request to Mrs. Frances Elizabeth Longfellow, who is said to have received many a letter from female admirers of her husband begging one long hair from his beautiful beard. If she had yielded to every request, the poet would have had no beard left to be admired. Fortunately things have changed and are still changing. In the days of Longfellow, though it is only a hundred years or so ago, the population of America was not big, and things did not move swiftly in all directions. People had time to admire poetry or a poet's beard. Nowadays the birthrate of America is very high, and activities in all fields are numerous and speedy. Many famous men and women could be admired every day. One just does not know whom to admire and cannot be bothered through lack of time. Therefore, poets of the present day and their families are left in peace.

The people of Cambridge used to be very fond of walking, and they used to walk to Boston for lectures and for shopping. Nowadays motor cars and other means of transport give them more time to do other things. Have they done more valuable things? They have lost the art of walking. Not many people are seen walking on Brattle Street now. My favourite walk in Cambridge is along the river-front. Though the dashing mobile cars on Memorial Drive have chased away the tranquil air, I quite like moving slowly, sitting on the benches now and then, and gazing at Beacon Hill on the other side of the Charles from the grassy shore in front of the main entrance of the Massachusetts Institute of Technology. I think the directors of M.I.T. were wise to find new ground for the building of the Auditorium and the Chapel, some distance from the main group of buildings, which are unique. No contrast is noticeable, spaced as they are, and each group can be appreciated for itself.

Once I was walking with Yang Lien-sheng along the riverfront when suddenly we came upon a big squarish stone by the corner of a private garden, with the following words engraved on it:

> On this spot
> in the year 1000
> Leif Ericson
> built his house in
> Vineland.

This caused us both to smile. I remarked that Ericson must have come to build his house about the beginning of our Sung dynasty. There is a big Ericson monument erected on Commonwealth Avenue. How, then, could Columbus claim he was the first European to land in America? How could the Pilgrims say that they were the first group to reach Boston? The Bostonians claim that United States art, music, literature, and history all began in Boston. Lien-sheng retorted: What about the spot where there used to be a big elm tree on Cambridge Common under which George Washington *first* took command of the American army? I laughed but said nothing.

I prefer to walk along the river shore between the two small brick bridges, behind the various houses of Harvard

University in the early morning. One Sunday morning in May I managed to get there about seven o'clock. I could never have believed that that small area of land could be so quiet. The air was delicious, pure, and cool; the sky was

almost cloudless, the sun was already up. I trod on fresh green grass. From nowhere a few pigeons gathered round my feet, cooing in turns to greet me, as I thought. Being a man like most men, I first had a suspicion that they were begging food from me and I felt quite sorry to have none to offer them. A second look showed me that they were pecking happily in the grass and not concerned with me at all. I suppose we human beings incline to wonder what others want of us rather than what we could do for others. Had I had some food with me and thrown it to the ground, the pigeons would undoubtedly have pecked at it, but they gave no sign of begging. They just liked my company. I then stepped upon the small red-brick bridge and stood on it, gazing at the water, which looked so still, although some little leaves and broken twigs floated from under the arch of the bridge. Clusters of reeds grew on both sides at intervals, the near ones tall and clear. Such was the magic vision of my eyes, but not the reality of my sophisticated knowledge as a modern man. I do not reject reality, but I do enjoy the magic vision of my eyes. Delighted with the scene, I wandered over to the other bank and continued my movement on the soft, velvety grass of the field. Some more pigeons had come to enjoy my company. Other birds flew by without letting me recognize them. But a pair of swallows shot down and skimmed away again. Something had set the reeds near me shaking. I continued my stroll and it brought me past the reeds. All of a sudden two pairs of ducks rose up and flew away over the river, then up and up to make a circle in the air above the tree-tops by the buildings of the Harvard University. I reproached my carelessness in disturbing them, but enjoyed my good fortune, for, as my eyes followed the flight of the ducks, they seemed to point out to me here the red tower of Eliot House, there the blue one of Lowell House, further right the emerald tower of Dunster House, and the golden tower of Adams House. Each seemed to have been cut out of coloured paper and ingeniously pasted on the clear, pale sky. There was a mysterious subtlety in the blend of colours. Something like a morning sunny haze softened and veiled the sharpness of the outlines and the crude face value of the individual colours as well: Above all this placidity there was something communicable, something serving to accentuate the solitude and stillness of the whole scene from the little red-brick bridge, the river, the grass field, the trees, and the red-brick buildings of the University. I had not before understood the reasons for having different colours for the towers. Now I did, thanks to the ducks. Before a single automobile had appeared on the road by the river I was back breakfasting with the Yangs.

XV

Boston Immortals

T H O U G H "immortal" is an English word, it does not often
appear in my English reading. It seems to me that it has
lost its existence in the minds of English-speaking people. I
may quite likely be wrong about this. On the other hand,
this word has now a perpetual Chinese association, for it
has been used to translate the Taoist term *hsien-jen,* which
bears some resemblance to a Western saint or angel. However, in the Chinese Taoist mythology a *hsien-jen* or an
immortal is not usually a young, handsome or charming
supernatural being, but instead a number of them are quite
old persons who originally lived as earthly beings, but by
their research in elixirs and by their attainments in the
study of the inner secret of life became supernatural, never
dying. Without need of food or clothes or shelter they live
in the Taoist paradise, roaming here and there in heaven
and riding the clouds to keep watch over the human world,
in case they are needed to come down and give their help,
by healing sickness or easing sufferings. There are eight
Taoist immortals, one of whom is a young lady and another
a lame beggar. They have been represented in all forms
of Chinese art—I mean, in painting, in jade-carving, wood-
carving, textiles, lacquer, and also in porcelain. Not only
are they entirely free from human worries and from earthly
death, but they possess magical and divine power, and we
have many legends about their miracles. Most of the Chinese,
from emperor down to beggar, have had their dreams of

becoming an immortal. I believe many must still have such
a dream. Only, at the moment the human world is suffering
a great catastrophe such as occurs every several hundred years
according to Taoist faith, and which it is beyond the eight
Immortals' power to avert.

My choice of the word "immortal" for the Boston big men
of the past is not because I think they possessed magical and
divine power and could perform miracles, but because I
feel that they seem to be still alive in Boston. By the perpetual existence of her past notables, Boston has been and
is still a unique city in America and indeed in the world,
for I have never known so many notables born within such
a small area of land on earth, each to play his part directly
or indirectly in the production of a hybrid civilisation of
mankind in our present epoch.

Having stayed in Boston for a while, I began to be interested in the verses engraved on tombstones of the seventeenth
to the second half of the nineteenth century. Epitaph-writing
has been one of the chief professions for noted men of
letters throughout the history of China, and it is a special
type of Chinese literature. The epitaphs were written in
eulogistic prose; a large number of them exist still in books,
but most have little value, though they are beautifully
composed. The New England tombstone verses reached their
height in the American Civil War and many of those I have
read show the early-American sense of humour. I was told
that that period is regarded as the weeping-willow period
of American literature.

One sunless but bright afternoon I was standing by the
big tombstone in the center of the Granary Burying Ground,
reading the following words:

> Josiah Franklin and his wife Abiah lie here interred.
> They lived lovingly together in wedlock

fifty-five years, and without an estate or any
gainful employment, by constant labor and
honest industry maintained a large family
comfortably, and brought up thirteen children
and seven grandchildren respectably. From
this instance, reader, be encouraged to diligence
in thy calling, and distrust not Providence.
   He was a pius and prudent man;
   She a discreet and virtuous woman.

A middle-aged, broad-shouldered man in a fine summer suit
came up and asked me if that was Benjamin Franklin's tomb.
I said "no," presuming that he could not be bothered to
read the inscription. He then told me that he came from
Louisiana and that he had read of Franklin's birthplace in
Boston, so thought he might have been buried in Boston
too. So far he had not succeeded in finding the tombstone.
I immediately recalled what I had read of Benjamin Franklin's will: "No monumental display for me."

Born in Boston, 1706; died on Philadelphia, in 1790, was buried
in Christ Churchyard, Philadelphia.

Some years before his death he wrote his own epitaph:

> The body of
> Benjamin Franklin, Printer,
> like the cover of an old book,
> its contents torn out,
> And stript of its lettering and gilding,
> lies here, food for worms.
> Yet the work itself shall not be lost,
> For it will appear once more
> in a new
> and a more beautiful edition.

Franklin's greatness in the years of the American Revolution
and his part in the universal science of electricity make

Boston proud to have been his birthplace and Philadelphia proud to be his resting place.

In the same burial ground lie the graves of three signers of the Declaration of Independence—John Hancock, Samuel Adams and Robert Treat Paine. The sight of Paul Revere's name on a tombstone took me to see the oldest building in Boston, where he lived for thirty years, 1770–1800, married

Paul Revere House from back Yard

twice and had eight children by each wife. I heard someone say that the little Reveres used to pack their father's finished silverware in the saddle bags which hang in one of the rooms of the house for him to deliver to his country customers. There were many things on show which came from the skillful hands of Paul Revere—silver ladles, teaspoons, flagons, braziers, sugartongs, etc.—all in fine taste and of good design. I also saw cannon balls made by Revere. The house was a wooden structure with the big fireplace in the parlor breathing the very air of an old English country house. Quite likely it had a few neighbours when it was built some two hundred years ago. I followed others upstairs. I saw a few odd news sheets which were said to have been printed by Paul Revere, but could not find the following passage which I read somewhere in a book:

. . . hearty young woman with a good young breast of milk, that can be well recommended . . . would go into a gentleman's family to suckle.

However, this must have referred to the hiring of a wet-nurse, a common practice in China until very recently, but I never remember seeing an advertisement like that in my home-town. I was myself brought up by a wet-nurse till I was three, for my mother became ill after my birth.

Paul Revere was the first dentist to practice in the United States of America. It is said that after the battle of Bunker Hill, Paul Revere identified the body of General Warren by an artificial tooth and the wire that he had used to fasten it in. What interested me more was an advertisement Revere put in a newspaper of 1768:

Whereas, many Persons are so unfortunate as to lose their Fore-Teeth by Accident, and otherways, to their great Detriment, not only in Looks, but speaking both in Public and Private:—This is to inform all such, that they may have them re-placed with artificial Ones, that looks as well as the Natural, and answers the End of Speaking to all Intents, by Paul Revere.

His reasons are sound and convincing. Could this not be the forerunner of the art of publicity, advertisement, and salesmanship, that excels in America today?

Time is a factor that everybody in America is aware of nowadays. How Revere managed to accomplish so much must remain a secret. I learn that he cast seventy-five of the sweetest bells which are still in use in churches and in town-halls in America today. He also engraved the first paper money to be circulated in America. He rolled sheets of copper for the dome of the State House of Massachusetts, which was then gilded and shines in the Boston sun on Beacon Hill today. He did, too, many beautifully-carved wooden frames for Copley's paintings. It is safe to say that he made a success of everything he tackled. He is a sort of Boston Leonardo da Vinci, a man of many-sided talent, although, unlike Leonardo, of no specific training. Paul Revere played little part in shaping the birth of America, after his famous ride. I am not in a position to suggest that his educational background was not impressive, but it is my fancy to imagine that it did not impel his friends of the time to push him into the foreground with the Continental army or with Washington, even in a minor capacity.

The name of Paul Revere came to my notice through Longfellow's poem about his memorable ride. I learnt later that Prescott and Dawes also rode on the same night as Revere, but Longfellow did not dramatise what they did. Literature is the chief flower of any country's civilisation; and it is her literature that makes the history of the country known to other parts of the world and immortalizes her greatness. Paul Revere's historic deed will undoubtedly continue to be known to every generation of New Englanders and American citizens at large. Longfellow's poem made me pay a visit to the Old North Church, too, which I noted is the oldest church in Boston, built in 1723. It was as spotless inside as if it was a modern structure. The signal lantern of Paul Revere, displayed in the steeple of this church on April 18, 1775, was the central object of attention for all visitors. The sexton also showed us the old communion chest of the church, which was recently found.

A Common Sight at Thanksgiving Time

Faulkner Farm
(House of the American Academy of Arts and Sciences)

I then strolled to the Prado, a square behind the church
with a statue of Paul Revere on horseback in the middle of
it. To my surprise the square was full of people, men and
women, old and young, packed together on the benches so
that hardly a space was left. The youngsters were playing
ball while a few small groups of men played cards or chess.
I moved more slowly and watched the games. No one was
troubled by my presence. There was a homely feeling in
the air. I felt that I had strolled somewhere outside Boston,
for the language being used was beyond my intelligence. I
then learned that this was now the Italian quarter of the
city. Despite the Italian atmosphere, the immortality of
Paul Revere marks it as still Boston.

Longfellow pushed me round Boston after Paul Revere.
Longfellow lured me to see his own house along Brattle
Street in Cambridge. And he also sent me to pay the Wayside
Inn a visit. Curiously enough, I knew Longfellow when I
was a schoolboy in China some forty years ago. In the beginning of the present century not many Chinese students
came to study in America. But those few who had the chance
to come and study became important figures in the then
so-called modernised Chinese educational field. They decreed
Washington Irving's *Sketch Book* and some of Longfellow's
poems, together with a few noted English writers, to be
the necessary requirements for reading in English, if one
hoped to go and study abroad. Despite the struggle of all
the young fellows for the mere understanding of a single
word in the reading material, Longfellow and Irving became
great names in China for those who were trying to learn
a little English. During my first visit to America in 1946,
I hardly heard anyone mention Irving or Longfellow. Now
many even sneer at the mention of the latter's poems. Our
present age tends to be international in outlook. Neverthe-

less, Longfellow stands immortal in the area of Boston and in the heart of those who care about the history of American literature.

Longfellow's house not only gave me an idea of the elegant-looking, dignified white-and-yellow walls and the dormered and balustraded roof of the old buildings of New England, but also made me feel how much Longfellow, the poet, must have enjoyed his life in such an ideal residence. One morning I stood in the secluded meadow-ground by the house surrounded with the high hedge of lilacs, dreamingly seeing the poet in his old age sitting in the balcony at the back of the house in contemplation of some fine lines. Good poetry could still be written there without disturbance from outside. Brattle Street is still the best long street for a peaceful morning walk in Cambridge.

Donald Messenger implemented my visit to the Wayside Inn. We set out after a beautiful sunset which gave warm colour to the earth, although it was a very chilly February evening. No other car was on the road. Donald told me that the former road leading past the front of the Wayside Inn was a highway and that people just rushed by on it in their automobiles without turning their head to give the old building a look. The late Henry Ford, who had bought the whole plot of land including the inn, built a new mile-long road to divert traffic from it, which cost more than the inn and the land. Absent-mindedly, I joked that that must have spoilt the name "Wayside." But I discovered that it was still the Wayside Inn. While our car approached the gate of the inn, on the other side of the road stood a thin figure holding a long pole and trying to light the gas lamp as if in a picture of olden days. My friend beamed happily, saying that that was worth while seeing. "Would the man light the lamps on a very cold, snowy evening?"

I inquired. "Yes," was the answer, for Mr. Ford wished in his will that everything should be kept as it was in Longfellow's day. Indeed, everything inside the inn was *spotlessly kept*, and the electric bulbs in the lanterns were dim to ensure the two-hundred-year-old atmosphere. A young lady clerk was sitting on a desk reading *A Streetcar Named Desire*. No tablecloths nor silver were on the tables, which let me guess that no travellers were staying in the inn. Longfellow never foresaw how much trouble he was giving to the agents of the restorer. His single line about the fireplace that "touched Princess Mary's pictured face, and crowned the somber clock with flame" cost the agents one whole year in finding that picture of Princess Mary. Another year's hunt brought the "somber clock" made in London in the reign of Victoria and lacquered in black on the death of the illustrious queen.

Not far away from the inn stands an old mill, which was also restored by Mr. Ford. The mill grinds wheat and corn as it did in Colonial days. I sat on the stone wall to make a rough sketch while Donald took a photograph of me and the mill. It was too dark for us to go and see the inside of the mill, nor did we see the Old School House, where "Mary Had a Little Lamb" was recited. I reflected that American cartoonists have undoubtedly not been given a chance to show their talent in cracking a joke or two about the "ruin-hunters," as do English and Scottish cartoonists.

I learned that the aged Ralph Waldo Emerson attended the funeral of Longfellow on the arm of Charles Eliot Norton and died only a month later. Longfellow and Emerson had a great affection for each other.

Why do Longfellow's poems not breathe much international feeling when his knowledge was so international? I think "time" is the chief factor controlling the area of thought and feeling. In Longfellow's time the area covered by thought and feeling was Europe, and in America now we think and feel more on a global basis. At any rate, Longfellow could never have dreamed that I would come to Boston and write something about him.

Emerson, too, was highly internationally-minded as far as I can understand him from his writings. His *Representative Men* concerns all men everywhere. His doctrine of Self-reliance was practiced by himself and has been practiced by many other men in many other lands without a specific term to describe what they were doing. When he was only nineteen, Emerson had a wonderful dream or a most-ahead-of-time vision for the future; he wrote in 1822: "New Romes are growing, and the Genius of man is brooding over the wide boundaries of infinite empires, where yet are to be drunk the intoxicating drafts of honor and renown; here are to be played over again the bloody games of human ambition, bigotry, and revenge, and the stupendous Drama of the passions to be repeated. Other Cleopatras shall seduce, Alexanders fight, and Caesars die." These few words, noted in his journal at a rather young age, showed his great vision of a world which may well be the one we are living in now. Unfortunately, in his Harvard College days he had a definite area limit for his thought, that is, he was dreaming of the greatness of America. It is said that Emerson used to tend his widowed mother's cow on Boston Common and learned the ways of cows by becoming a patient, practical, and kindly philosopher. Long after his cowherd days, Emerson saw a young man struggling to get a tender calf through a wooden gate, pushing, pulling and pulling, pushing to no avail. Coming forward, Emerson, already famous, gently told the young man not to beat the calf but instead he tucked a finger into a corner of the calf's mouth, which made the tender creature suck hard and trot along quietly. This little story alone would make Emerson a universally loved man in the countryside of all countries.

While Emerson was living in Concord, Thoreau was in his company frequently and Emerson had much to say about him, whom "the animal would itself go toward . . . in fearless curiosity, to watch the watcher!" Thoreau was a hermit, with ideas of his own. Yet at times he would leave his "so companionable companion" as he called the chair "Solitude" he made himself for his hut. And how fortunate that he had friends who could understand him, like Emerson, Hawthorne, and others. When I travelled in Edinburgh years ago, I was constantly reminded that the Scottish capital was fortunate in having produced so many noted men of letters and that David Hume, Sir Walter Scott, and Robert Louis Stevenson used to gather round a nice fire and tell stories to each other in the building, now the National Library of Scotland. When I think of Longfellow, Emerson, Thoreau and many others as contemporaries living outside and inside Boston, I find this city similarly fortunate.

Nevertheless, Thoreau's hut by the shore of Walden Pond is not so fortunate as the Wayside Inn. It did not have a wealthy neighbour to restore it for visitors. Undoubtedly Thoreau's idea of making life of equal simplicity and innocence with Nature herself would be hard to represent in restoration. One morning in March I went with Arthur Walworth to try to locate where Thoreau's hut must have been by the Walden Pond. A small part of the pond shore was paved for a swimming pool and dotted with bathing cabins near the main road. It was still cold when we were there, nobody about, and trees bare. Arthur took the lead, for he wanted to show me the old railway track first. He understood that Thoreau's hut was built not far from it. We walked on all the possible footpaths and trotted along now on big pebbles, now on mud. Heavy rain had fallen there the night before. We were never far away from the pond and most of the time along its shore. A very thin morning mist was dispersing slowly, revealing in the water the reflection of the purplish hue among the tree-tops on the slope of the other side of the pond. The water surface was mirror-like, except when some invisible little creature, perhaps a green frog, tried to come through it but only managed to make a bubble. There was warmth down in the bottom of the pond, and in the air too. Chickadees—such friendly American little birds, which have long roused my affection in the same way as British robins—accompanied us all the way, while a pair of swallows seemed to have come very early from the south, and were skimming over the water now and then. Though the trees were all bare, young green leaves opened their eyes to peep at us here and there. The woods, full and luxurious, did not seem to have changed much from Thoreau's days when he sat watching them some hundred years ago. I do not know why the land around the Walden Pond has remained more or less untouched. Was it by public consent in memory of Thoreau? Or by the mere slow development which might spread from the small area of swimming-pool quarters and bathing cabins? We had come to a point of the shore from which we could not see the modernised part. No sign of Thoreau's hut was to be found; not even a stone tablet marking the spot. My friend felt that it was a great pity. I thought it unnecessary, perhaps, for any tablet to be there. I felt that we were in Thoreau's company in spirit that morning. From the little I have read about Thoreau, I understand that he was not much liked by his contemporaries and was dubbed "skulker," simply because he lived by withdrawing to a vantage-point by the Walden

Pond that was half-hermitage and half-ambush, yet not far from the smell of his mother's cooking. But I think his work *Walden*, apart from his other writings, represents a unique piece of writing to induce people to be interested in a small area of nature and life—unique, for no one could live such a life nowadays. Thoreau's integrity as a man of one idea for life is unquestionable to me.

One evening I attended a small, informal gathering between Cambridge and Boston, such as I had often attended in Oxford, England. Yet there was a difference, in that the talk always brought in something about the Bostonians. Actually there were a few Bostonians in the gathering, though I could not tell which were and which were not. Someone remarked that Thomas Bailey Aldrich, author of the famous *Story of a Bad Boy*, once said of himself, "Though I am not genuine-Boston, I am Boston-plated." Another numbered four qualifications for a genuine-Bostonian: (1) having a share in the Boston Athenaeum, (2) having once lived in and had a family house on Beacon Hill, (3) having a subscription to the Boston Symphony Orchestra Concerts, and (4) having a relative buried in the Mount Auburn Cemetery. The last qualification led me to Cambridge the next morning.

As I passed through the main entrance, a uniformed person came to offer me help. I was struck by his most friendly manner. He said "Life is so short. We must try to help to make life more interesting to one another." He then gave me a map of the cemetery and told me to follow him into a brownstone building, the chapel. Inside he unlocked many shelves on the walls of the crypt, revealing rows of small, shiny metal boxes containing the ashes of the deceased. I asked if there was any dust of Boston geniuses there. The answer was "surely," but that the most famous dust was scattered round the gardens. It did not take me long to find out his interest in me, or, say, in my flat face. He told me that on Thanksgiving day (six months before I came) a Chinese family of five brought with them an enormous turkey, candles, joss-sticks and other things he did not recognise, in various dishes. They then poured some white wine into three small cups, lit some firecrackers and the incense, and kowtowed or knelt down three times in front of a grave in which an aged Chinaman had been buried a year before. He expressed great admiration for the family, for every one of the five looked serene and full of reverence for the deceased. "It is not often one sees young people showing so much regard for the old dead," he added. I explained that that must have been the anniversary of the one buried in the grave, and that it was the old Chinese custom for every member of the family to pay him homage. But I wondered why a countryman of mine was buried in Mount Auburn Cemetery. So I asked how it was possible. He said that there were many new plots available and told me to go and have a look at the Chinese grave. Before we parted he told me that his ancestors came from Sweden but that he himself was born and bred in Boston. He also told me to look for the *small* tombstones of the big men of Boston and Cambridge. I said I did not know many big names but would try to follow his advice.

Not far from the Chapel, under a dark-coloured stone, I found the name of James Russell Lowell. I know him as the first editor of *The Atlantic Monthly*, founded in 1857, with a high standard for every article published. That standard is still upheld today. A story that made me remember Lowell well is the one told by Emerson in 1868: "at a meeting of the Saturday Club, when the copies of *The Atlantic Monthly* were brought in, everyone rose eagerly to get a copy, and then each sat down, and *read his own article*." At that time the contributors to *The Atlantic Monthly* were chiefly Bostonians. How like the descendants of Boston families today who go to the Museum of Fine Arts at Huntington Avenue only to gaze at the family portraits of their own family! I wonder if the descendants of the Lowells come to see only their ancestors' tombs in Mount Auburn Cemetery. Many names of different Lowells came to my eyes afterwards. The other name I knew was Amy Lowell, for I have been told that she was a buxom lady, often having a big black cigar in her mouth while writing her passionate, beautiful poems. This is the perfect opposite to the Chinese conception of a poetess as a delicate, slender female with hardly the strength to hold the brush. Amy Lowell may easily have been the first woman to smoke cigars. What did other Bostonian women think of her?

I went up a few steps to a meadow slope on Indian Ridge Path where I found the single tombstone of Longfellow. Why were there no other Longfellows? Was Longfellow, the poet, a genuine Bostonian?

The contrast became greater when I encountered many Holmeses on Lime Avenue. One of them was Oliver Wendell Holmes.

Holmes' description of "Little Boston" in *The Professor at the Breakfast Table* is still the pride of most Bostonians nowadays: "full of crooked little streets; but I tell you Boston has opened, and kept open, more turnpikes that lead straight to free thought and free speech and free deeds than any other city of live men or dead men,—I don't care how broad their streets are, nor how high their steeples!"

Water always attracts me. Presently I was moving round Halcyon Lake. There was massive, oppressive green all round, for the trees and plants were all overgrown. It was on the way to summer. Fortunately red cottage roses and other gay flowers on trellises and in the flower-beds helped to take away something of the oppressiveness. So did the water-lilies on the lake and the yellow flags round the edge of it. I sat on a bench for a while, gazing at the stillness of the water with a feeling that I was back in Kew Gardens, London. The scene that lay immediately in front of me was not unlike the small pond in Kew, but the surroundings were not wide-open enough to keep one's heart light. Mount Auburn Cemetery is the only and the oldest garden cemetery in America. It was consecrated in 1831 when people thought it a novelty. At first it must have been more a garden than a cemetery. Emerson used to take his students there, and they soon lost themselves in solitary contemplation on its shady walks. It was known that James Russell Lowell often wandered through Mount Auburn's glades seeking inspiration for his poetry. When Franklin Pierce was lost in thought under a tree along Bellwort Path or Spruce Avenue, he received the message that he had been nominated to the Presidency of America. Charles Dickens was directed to this garden cemetery. Emperor Dom Pedro of Brazil, followed by his large retinue, had a look. And Edward VII, as Prince of Wales, planted a purple beech tree here in 1860. I have not found it so far. Many more notabilities have come to Boston since then, but few have paid Mount Auburn a visit. There are more learned professors and contemplative students at Harvard than before, yet very few set foot in Mount Auburn for inspiration and thought. The change is perhaps because Mount Auburn is now more a cemetery than a garden. The beauty of Mount Auburn has not changed from the days when Emerson, Lowell, and others admired it so much, but the presence of too many tombstones, in increasing number yearly, has changed its character. The growth of population changes not only the character of Mount Auburn but that of human society and also that of the history of nations. Our present age is different from the past, owing to the growth of population everywhere. Can we solve the ensuing problems? I wonder . . .

Collecting my straying thoughts, I got up to examine the reflection of a domeless, Greek-temple-like structure in

Halcyon Lake

Halcyon Lake. Then I made my way to the temple itself and found it to be the tomb of Mary Baker Eddy, founder of Christian Science. She occupies a beautiful spot. The Pilgrims who came to Boston shores had passed through all difficulties. The Pilgrims' spirit has filled the air of Boston ever since. Mrs. Mary Baker Eddy represents the Pilgrims' spirit, to my thinking.

I moved along many paths and the long Spruce Avenue until I found the tomb of my compatriot, whose name is Tseng Chuan-hsi, a native of T'ai-Shan, Kuangtung Province. There is plenty of room in the new part of the cemetery. I recalled how David McKibbin had told me that when Henry James was about to be buried in Mount Auburn, the city paid no heed to the event, for James had lived most of his lifetime in England and had attacked his own country for having kept aloof from the First World War. Perhaps even fewer people will pay heed to any event in Mount Auburn now, no matter who is being buried.

Longfellow Bridge

Seagulls cease to cry over the Charles' shiny water;
Ducklings drowsily break into occasional quacks.
The noisy cars, coming and going, do not disturb
    my ears;
Lights along Beacon Hill are twinkling.
My heart is carefree, night tranquil;
    I drink the pure breeze,
Greedily watching the moon above Longfellow Bridge.

長人橋
漁翁胡詩

鷗鳥水面醫聲歇
小鴨欲眠時唶之街
車來往往若夢聞
筆耕山側燈明滅心
閒夜靜飲清風貪
看長人橋上月

XVI

Boston Dragon

THE DRAGON is an animal everyone has heard of, but what kind of animal it is is anybody's guess. Neither Aristotle nor Darwin made any statement about it. Nevertheless, a dragon in the eyes of Europeans and probably of all Bostonians is a monster which has to be disposed of or be kept out of sight, whereas in Chinese eyes it is friendly and benevolent and can control wind, rain, and thunder. Therefore it was the symbol of the imperial power, and the former imperial robes of China were adorned with dragon emblems all over.

Had one of the early English settlers heard of a dragon in or around Boston, he might, I am sure, have drawn his sword to emulate Saint George. But I think Bostonians during the prosperous China-trade period got used to dragons, for they saw many of them as decoration on the Chinese *objets d'art* which they or their ancestors brought back from China. They may even have had kind feelings towards dragons as symbols of imperial power, for Bostonians were the aristocrats of America. The following words from a son of Boston, Alan Priest, Curator of the Department of Far Eastern Art at the Metropolitan Museum of Art support my statement:

Compare a medieval dragon with a Chinese dragon. Both are fantastic, but ever and always your Chinese dragon and all the other beasts are logical creatures. The Western dragon is a lumpy, unwieldy creature, somewhat pinned together. The Chinese dragon out of glorious fish into a creature of air is far more logical, far more believable.

There is a dragon of Boston. It is naturally not alive. It is a petrified one. Why have no Harvard professors of ethnology or of archaeology ever found it? It has little to do with either ethnology or archaeology. It is not inside Boston. I came upon it when David McKibbin took me for a trip northward of Boston.

Chinese dragon

I had mentioned to McKibbin several times that I had tried to see Boston Harbor but had found no suitable viewpoint. He suggested the trip. I did not know where we were going. First we took the train for Lynn and then changed on to a bus, which seemed to be moving on a rope stretched over the blue water, for I could see the sea on both sides. The bus went on and on for a good while and I felt within me an expectation of something unusual. McKibbin was very considerate and travelled as silently as I. At last I followed him out of the bus and we went straight into Edgehill Inn where he hoped to find a friend who often stayed there. Although his friend was no longer there, the proprietor and his wife were soon engaged in deep conversation with McKibbin. I realised that we were on the island of Nahant, which is not really an island, as there is a long, narrow strip of land joining it to the mainland. Their talk was chiefly about old residents of Nahant. Many well-known Bostonian families with names such as Curtis, Motley, Otis, Amory, Lowell, Paine, Hammond, etc., had homes there. One of them married a foreign-titled woman who used to go out without hat and gloves and horrified her neighbours. Captain Sibias had Shelley's guitar; Henry James came in 1916; and so on. The proprietress poured all the names out as if she was going over her visitors' register. She must have been the oldest resident left on Nahant, for she said that very few representatives of the Bostonian families were to be found now, though their old homes were still on the island.

Presently we went through the hall and stood on the back balcony of the Inn to see Boston. McKibbin remembered that he had stood there with his friend on many an occasion before. A number of big trees grew below, and beyond them a wooden structure with a landing stage stretched into the sea. Round the landing stage were a few small sailing boats. The boats were bobbing up and down, I could see, but not a leaf of the trees under the balcony was vibrating. There was a saturated tranquillity in the air. Yet to right and to left I saw the furtive motion of the flowing tide. The water beyond the landing stage was deep blue, perhaps bluer than the sky above. Yet far, far away in the distance where Boston lay there was neither blue sky, nor blue water, but an edgeless sheet of soft white haze. Boston was hidden behind it and could not be perceived. McKibbin was disappointed, but I enjoyed the ancient inexplicable mystery of sun, water, and earth. We were on Nahant on September 23, 1953. September is known as the "Month of peace"; and I had not found a quieter place right in the sea around Boston.

McKibbin told me that on his former visits he and his friend had seen Boston very well, for the air over the long stretch of the sea could be extremely clear. They had even been able to see the winking of Boston lights.

Presently we came to a point called Forty Steps Bay. Before we walked down the steps McKibbin showed me the wild bayberries. The early Pilgrims made great use of bayberries chiefly for candles, for they contain wax material. I wondered if the Indians had ever used bayberries to make candles. Many small sumac trees had already turned red to denote that the Indian summer was not far from Nahant. The Egg Rock came in sight very clearly. It must have been a huge rock in the sea. How long had it been battered by the high waves to shape it into an egg in our eyes? And how long before its shape will be altered? From the Egg Rock our talk came to the so called thousand-years-preserved eggs of China. I do not remember how we then came to talk of the busy cruising round the caves and coves of the island and along all the coast near Boston in the Prohibition era. I remember well that in 1931–1932, American naval vessels used to steam up the Yangtse River and their captains or commanders paid official calls at my office of the Kiukiang District Government. They invited me to dine on their ships and I reciprocated the friendly gesture. One evening twelve American officers came to have a Chinese feast in the garden of my *yamen*. They all enjoyed the food enormously, but the Chinese yellow wine and other drinks including *pai-kan-êr* or *kao-liang-chiu* (spirit distilled from millet), appealed even more. After many rounds we strolled about the garden and drank still more; they did not care whether I emptied my glass each time or not. The last thing I remember is that we all had our arms round each others' necks, and were talking together in the friendliest possible way. But not a word they said could I understand! A basket full of bottles of yellow wine and some *pai-kan-êr* was ready for them as my parting present to give them further pleasure. The captain rolled out a few words, unintelligible to my ears, but my subordinate understood. It was an apologetic refusal with a grin. They were under "Prohibition"!

Suddenly I heard the cries of a flock of wild geese which had appeared from nowhere and were following their leader in the direction of Little Nahant. Autumn was in full swing. In Chinese literature the cry of the wild geese was always associated poetically with autumn, and their appearance marked the time for all travellers to be ready for the family gathering near the end of the year. I had heard the cries of wild geese in the British Isles for many years and I now heard them on Nahant. The old association has flashed into my mind each time but cannot be indulged, for home-coming is out of the question for me for the moment. However, I have new associations. Elizabeth Coatsworth (Mrs. Henry Beston), a noted poetess of many volumes, once wrote to me:

Henry called me out a minute ago to see a great flock of geese against the gray sky. They were hanging indecisive. A goose left the flock and came down into our cove, followed by five others (perhaps his family?), but the main flock, shouting and calling, straightened into their arrow and flew west, and after a little while the others followed, first the five, and at last the one, flying low, through the trees (was he wounded or tired?).

She did not intend me to answer her questions any more than the wild geese over Nahant were interested in the thoughts they roused in me. In my young days I loved to hear stories of shooting wild geese; later I enjoyed their poetic association and delighted to watch them in flight; and now perhaps I just observed them in flight with care for the purpose of portraying them in ink and color. I still paint them with pleasure. I made a good many rough sketches of wild geese in flight when I stayed with the Bestons at their

Chimney Farm a little way above a lovely lake in Nobleboro, Maine.

The bus between Lynn and Nahant ran only at long intervals, I was told. Very few cars were to be seen on any road. We saw no one as we moved along except an elderly man

Geese over lake of Chimney farm, Nobleboro, Maine

rocking his chair on the porch of a house. He did not disturb the air, but instead the stillness of the air seemed to be elastic and helped to keep the rocking chair in constant motion. How purple the roofs of the houses turned, shaded by the autumn trees under the blue sky. What satisfaction the bright sunny haze gave, softening the tones of the sharp-edged corners of the houses and whitening their colonial-style doorways; what richness of colour were the elms, the sumacs, the bayberries and other plants I did not know, and grass grew together on the rocky cliffs, disorderly to the human eye yet orderly in their own way. A seagull or two hung immeasurably high, looking like paper-cut or ivory-carved ornaments pasted on the vast serenity of blue, where not the smallest cloud was to be seen. How miraculously those immobile winged stars suspended themselves in the sky and what unspeakable peace they reflected down on the earth. About ninety per cent of Nahant is surrounded by water. It reminded me much of the Cornish or Devon coast, though much warmer at the time of the year than there.

Mrs. Cunningham once told me an incident of her sister's arrival at Mrs. Sears' house in Rome. The Italian butler said that Mrs. Sears was very sad indeed. He had asked Mrs. Sears whether she thought the scenery in Italy was good. Mrs. Sears would just answer: "Nothing is as good as Nahant." So the Italian wanted to find out from Mrs. Cunningham's sister what Nahant was, a child or a dog, to have made Mrs. Sears so sad. "A place to which one has not been is a place one knows little about," says a Chinese proverb. I can understand Mrs. Sears' sentiment for Nahant.

Loud laughter, chased by noisy chatter, woke me up from my thoughts. One of five young boys had slipped off the edge of the rock into the water. The rest tried to hold him while he climbed up. Perhaps it was a game. They were all laughing and soon chased each other again among the rocks. Their jumping around created a whirl of wind. All parts of the rocks seemed to be melting together into a single mass. After a while the boys plunged into the water to swim, and their chatter became fainter and fainter. I continued to gaze at the rocks. They were taking the shape of a dragon! I told McKibbin of my discovery. He kept up his Boston-Athe-

naeum manner, gave a gentle nod and said in a soft voice
as if not surprised at all that he had heard of the sea-serpent
rock and had come to see it before but that to tell the truth
he had not looked at it carefully. He also said that Lord
Camperdown, the fourth earl, came here in 1936 and cata-

Petrified dragon at Nahant

logued it in his books as "Snake Hill." The word "dragon"
was not mentioned. Perhaps McKibbin retained the blood
of his ancestors who came from the British Isles. While I
was making rough sketches of the rock, I noticed that the
body of the dragon was cut into several sections and remarked that someone must have killed this dragon long before Saint George disposed of his. My friend smiled slightly.
After all, a careful analysis of the Chinese dragon as it is
used in designs and ornaments shows it to have the mouth
of a tiger with the barbels of a catfish, the horns of a deer,
the body of a serpent with a crest running its entire length
—evidently suggested by the crest along the tail of the alli-
gator or crocodile—the scales of a carp, the legs of a lizard,
and the talons of an eagle or possibly of the large water

monitor (*Varanus salvator*) found in South China. From the look of the petrified dragon along the Nahant shore there were many parts missing owing to age and the tide of the sea, I guessed. But it was a dragon to me. So Boston has a dragon, a petrified dragon.

XVII

Boston Heat

THERE used to be many grim stories about Gloucester. The sea can be calm and lovely there in summer, but it has its rough days. In the past the townfolk of Gloucester went off in their fishing boats over the sea, and they did not know when they would be back or if they would be back at all. Generation after generation they went off, keeping their sweethearts and brides waiting and waiting for their reappearance, sometimes in vain. Therefore Gloucester earned the name "city of sorrow, whose history is written in tears." However, it did not look to me a "city of sorrow" now. Though the sea may still be lashed to a rage under massive black clouds, the modern fishing folk have better and speedier vessels. Sweethearts and brides need not be so anxious. This proves that the present world is a better world than the past. There were many people in the town while I was there with Walter Whitehill and Paul Gray. We managed to find standing space in a little restaurant by the sea and had coffee and a piece of cake. Afterwards I made a quick sketch of a girl busying herself with the colorful buoys of wood for lobstering. Young Jane Whitehill, Walter's elder daughter (now Mrs. William Rotch), told me she found lobstering as easy as drawing water from a well, although the big claws of the creature were quick to clasp one's finger.

While my thoughts were pursuing the lobster there, Walter and Gray were talking to each other, waiting for me to finish my sketch. We then walked round Bass Rocks, where

we saw a number of huge wooden structures covered with
sheets so that they looked like shields in the distance. We
came to the conclusion that it must be fishing nets spread out
to air.

We skipped much of Gloucester, as Walter wanted us to
see the artists' colony at Rockport. We walked through a
narrow street, which was lined on both sides with shops selling curios and *objets d'art*. We had a look at the exhibition
in Rockport Art Association. But we found more art shows
in Bear Skin Neck, which was named after a bear caught
there by the tide and killed in 1700. Many artists were busy
at work and it seemed that every one was either a painter or
a potter. Gray stuck to his interest in plants and Walter had
much to say to him about gardening. I moved slowly round
the drawings in order to be fair to each artist. Unexpectedly
one drawing detained me longer than the others and also
made me chuckle to myself. It was a sketch of a sturdy man
in uniform, maybe a policeman or a coastal guard, which
happened to be pinned on the door of a shop. Involuntarily
the following Chinese joke came to my mind:

A certain constable had a rather amorous wife who had to
be carefully watched at all times. One day before he went on
duty, as a warning to intruders he painted on the left-hand
side of the door of their house a picture of a constable on
guard. He marked every position very carefully. When a
lover of the lady came along, he amused himself rubbing out
the picture on the left and drawing a similar one on the
right-hand side of the door. After returning from duty the
constable-husband immediately noticed the change. He was
enraged and shouted: "What I drew was on the left-hand
side of the door; how can it have moved to the right side?"
"I am astonished at your lack of knowledge after all your

years in the police force," replied the wife with a gentle smile, "have you never heard of 'changing the guard'?"

When I caught up with Walter and Gray we had to find a place to eat our lunch, which Jane Whitehill had so well prepared for us. Suddenly a big noise occurred at the rocky edge of the sea, for the bigger of two motor-boats capsized while being chased, as it looked from a distance, by a much smaller one. Two men struggled in the water for a good while before they got hold of a rock to climb up. They were loudly cheered by the onlookers.

After our lunch we stopped at Pigeon Cove—a settlement —which is a part of Rockport. There were quite a number of small yuccas in bloom. Walter mentioned that he and Paul Gray had a standing joke about this plant's ability to grow in unpromising spots despite all discouragement. Yucca is a rarity in the British Isles but quite common along the northern shore of Boston. Plants distinguish one place from another. The world of man has become *uniformized* day by day in clothes, food, and housing, but Nature insists on keeping one piece of earth different from another by the growth of different plants. I learned that yucca is a genus of lili-aceous trees and shrubs exclusively confined to North and Central America. Its foliage is essentially of a subtropical character, which, combined with a peculiar stateliness and beauty of flower, lends great decorative value to the coastal scenery which we were gazing at. Summer around the Boston shore is subtropical.

Around Ipswich Bay, Walter looked hard for a footpath to a particular place he had in mind for us to see. The path was found and we rambled down, down a slope for a good while. Grass and wild flowering plants as tall as ourselves lined both sides of the path. Peeping through them we saw some scraps of an old car scattered about on a field and an old shingled cottage surrounded by bright hollyhocks and trumpet-vines, and roses in the distance. The sun was high, the heat great, and nothing stirred in the field under the wide-open eyes of the hollyhocks. It was blazing hot farther down the valley, windless, with fierce sun baking my shoulders. We had come to a part of the path overgrown with trees and shrubs. Passing through the thicket we came out suddenly to a wide-open edgeless sea. The surprise was too great and I had to shut my eyes for a minute. Knocking out the ashes from his pipe, Walter remarked: "Here you are. This is Halibut Point Reservation. There is no house in sight and none will be built here. Few people come this way."

Masses of huge rocks lay close to one another and many more were piled on top. The area they covered was immeasurable and they faced us expressionless. They had been there since time immemorial and we to them were any living creature in any moment of time. Gray stretched his whole body on one of them; Walter stood on another relighting his pipe; and I jumped from one to another as far as I could see the view in a long stretch. There was a magic in the sea air. The sunshine was as bright as ever and the heat was undiminished, yet I no longer felt baked. Instead I was drunken with the scene and particularly with the exhilaration of the spotless blue above and the expanse of the green, flecked with white, and shimmering with silver. The fascination of emptiness liberated me from my ordinary habits of thinking and brought me close to the essence of Zen (Chinese Buddhism, called *Ch'an* in Chinese but now popularly known in the West by the Japanese term *Zen*) in seeing the nature of my own being—a being free of any bondage at that moment. Gray's body reclining in quiet contentment and Walter's motionless figure both accentuated the solitude and stillness of the whole surroundings. I did not want to jump any more; I sat down watching the sharp splash of the blue waves tossing their crests—they went on for no definite purpose and yet having no intention to stop.

There were too many waves moving and flowing, and rolling in front of me. Something obscure, something insignificant, something consistent and something formless—all gathered together to act with similar heart across countless leagues of the great sea. I began to see that I was getting on in years; I liked to ramble along on in my thoughts . . .

The sea air had done all three of us good. Gray got up and stretched his arms; Walter walked towards me, still smoking his pipe; and I made a few notes and a rough sketch. We returned to the same path and followed it back up the slope. None of us uttered a word. The shingled cottage with its hollyhocks, trumpet-vines and roses looked peaceful as the sun slanted towards the west. We reached a place named Folly Cove. I exclaimed at the name. Walter said that the inhabitants were very clever designers of fabrics which were sold under the name of the place in widely distant parts of the United States. Passing through Plum Cove, Annisquam, and rounding Planter's Neck, our car stopped at Ipswich, for Walter wanted to get a few postcards for me, but there were none for sale. I saw with amazement most of the waterfront full of sailing boats and motorboats. Gray remarked jokingly that I would tell all my English friends that every American had a boat.

On our way to Merrimack River I noticed a kind of herbal plant like a dandelion in shape but much bigger and with reddish flowers instead of yellow. Gray told me it was mullein, but he had not seen them growing so tall before. Mullein leaves are good for throat ailments.

After having seen Gray back to his home in Ward Hill,

we reached North Andover in time for dinner. After dinner, Walter took me for a stroll to the Old Burial Ground not far from his house, where he showed me an epitaph particularly appropriate to the occasion:

But we had not been melted.

Erected in memory of Mr. James Bridges
who departed this life July 17th, 1747,
in the 51st year of his age being
melted to death by extreme heat.

It was on exactly the same date, 206 years later, that we had encountered similar extreme heat. But we had not been melted. Our resistance towards heat may be better, but I am inclined to think that we were saved by the gaze at Halibut Point.

XVIII

Boston Fleet

WHEN I was walking along Marine Avenue in San Francisco where the lonely statue of the fabulous William C. Ralston stands in the center of the green, a man moved toward me and asked me to look at the clusters of masts where the faint image of the Golden Gate Bridge was just discernible. Jokingly he said: "There it is, the San Francisco fleet; every boat belongs to some wealthy man in San Francisco." When I saw masses of white sails along Marblehead harbor I thought they must be the "Boston fleet."

I do not know the New England coast well enough to express an opinion about it, but the parts of it which I have visited reminded me somewhat of the Cornish coast in England. Nevertheless, each of the Cornish towns retains its distinctive individuality, while the coastal towns of New England tend to be uniform. There is an outstanding exception and that is the town of Marblehead.

I had spent a fine day with Tseng Hsien-Ch'i in Marblehead, three years before the day I was taken to the Eastern Yacht Club for lunch. Hsien-Ch'i, a noted Chinese artist in Boston, who could seldom get away from his work at the Asiatic department of the Boston Museum of Fine Arts, telephoned to say that he would pick me up for a day's outing. We were soon driving in his car through the city along the most twisted, narrow streets that I have ever encountered in New England. I remarked that the streets seemed much narrower and more winding than in Boston. "Indeed, this is Marblehead, an ancient town," was the response from Hsien-Ch'i.

Each little lane on the north side of the high street leads down to the waterfront. We came to the most popular spot on the front. Huge rocks rose in strange shapes out of the sea, polished by the eternal washing of the waves. They looked naturally artistic to my eyes, although many might not agree with me. At least the artist, Nature, would consider my remark a little too hasty perhaps, for no great artist really feels satisfied with what he creates. He never ceases hoping to improve his work. Nature was still polishing those massive rocks before my eyes, but not the part of them where we were sitting—or, indeed, half-lying—nor other parts where a number of young girls and boys were jumping about, though no doubt her work of polishing was being carried on far down below gently and slowly. The Marblehead sun in June was quite warm. My palms enjoyed the smooth warm surface of the rock. I was gazing into the distance. At first glance the masses of yacht-sails lay before us in a shimmering obscured beauty, as in a Seurat painting, only with pure Chinese-white and no other pigments. Here and there were a few mistakenly dropped bright-red dots. By and by I noticed that the white dots of the sails were not so closely arranged as I had first thought, for there were dark green spaces in between them.

All the sails stood still; some beamed in the bright sun as if they were made of pure white satin, others were darkish and obscure in Shantung silk. On the other hand, the sun seemed tiptoeing on the sails' tops. A few seagulls were circling high above as they searched for spaces between the sails, where they could dive down for their food. Now six or seven sails moved off swiftly in a semicircle near my feet; it seemed as if they were about to turn over but they were

held firm by an invisible central force. I would not have
noticed them had it not been for the loud screeching of the
seagulls, whose peace of mind seemed to have been gravely
disturbed by the sudden appearance and disappearance of
the sweeping sails. Men could not have expressed their an-
noyance more clearly. Long after the sails had disappeared
the screeching went on. It is said that seagulls are real friends
of the fishermen out at sea, for they show them where to fish,
but I think the seagulls down below my feet were hostile
towards the yachtsmen, who had disturbed their fish. Life is
full of contradictions. The yachtsmen should not have poked
fun at the seagulls and the fish. Yet we, the onlookers on
the shore, watched with amusement the yachtsmen's daring
tactics. Then another whimsical thought came to me. The
still-screeching seagulls seemed to me to be like those house-
wives who scold their husbands for getting up late for break-
fasts and are still scolding when the husband has dashed off
to the office. It made me laugh. At the same time Hsien-Ch'i
laughed, though we did not exchange what we had in mind.

He said: "Let's go," and we rose quickly and set off towards a sandy path which was made around the edge of an
open space like a public park. The inner edge of the path
was lined with long wooden benches, each of which was fully
occupied. The scene behind the benches suggested a series
of old black silhouettes of the town in an age gone by. The
trees planted at almost equal intervals behind the benches
made the silhouette perfect in the old-fashioned manner.
The majority of those who sat there looked as if they belonged to the silhouette period and had come to bake themselves in the hard-earned sunshine after long experience of
life. Very few talked, and all were content in the light balmy
breeze that came up from the sea below and stirred the
leaves of the trees. I have never experienced so tranquil a

scene with so much commotion close at hand. These old people were all out to watch the rehearsal of the yachting regatta which was to be staged there very soon. They were all the town's folk, and there was no room for visitors. Marblehead must be unique in the United States in being owned and enjoyed by its inhabitants.

Tseng Hsien-Ch'i at Marblehead

We had to make full use of our day. The next spot we reached was the huge iron structure of the Marblehead Light House. The iron structure indicates how much older it is than others along the Maine and Massachusetts coasts. Many people were sitting on the lower iron bars and on the rocks not far away. The cliffs down to the water were perpendicular, and the water foamed as it beat against them in rhythmical tunes. A good many people were fishing here and there from the rocks round the small peninsula. Fish must have been plentiful. No sooner did one throw his line than a fish was pulled up, jumping and wriggling. Two sturdy young men, wearing shorts only, never seemed to miss a catch, and the sand behind them was strewn with fish, mostly sea-trout, I thought.

While my mind was pondering over fishing, my friend seemed to be in deep thought. At last he sighed and said: *"Sui hsin chih ch'u pu k'ê chung lai,"* or "A place where one's heart was once broken should not be revisited." This puzzled me, yet I could not enquire further for fear of increasing his sadness.

Now came my turn to suggest a move. It was St. John's Eve. I wanted to walk back to the main street and to see if the old houses of Marblehead had anything hung on their doors for that particular day. It is said that years ago people living along the English coast used to hang up branches of mugwort on their doors to keep away storm and the devil himself on Midsummer's Eve. Though the custom has long since died out in England, I thought some of the families who had settled in Marblehead might have handed down the tradition for tradition's sake. My friend did not encourage me in the idea. As we walked on, I saw a number of plants growing between the rocks. I thought I might find some fern there and experiment with the seeds, which if gathered on Midsummer Eve have magic properties. Those who wear them become invisible or so I had read in an old English book. When my friend heard what I was doing, he laughed at my old superstitious head. My comment was that whether superstitious or not I wished I could be invisible at that moment, so that I could study his moody behaviour without embarrassing him or myself. I received no reply except "Humph."

I also remember reading that on Midsummer Eve women try various modes of divination to discover their future lovers. One of them is to tie a garter nine times round the bedpost and tie nine knots in it, saying to oneself:

This knot I knit, this knot I tie,
To see my love as he goes by
In his apparel and array,
As he walks in every day.

It is said that after this spell the lover comes to tuck in the bedclothes at her feet and to draw the curtains. In China the young girl tied her girdle round the bedpost with three knots and three times only and said a Chinese poem. Is it not strange that there should be the same sort of superstition in two countries so far apart? Superstitions grew from the mysteries of life. When the mysterious are revealed, superstitions automatically vanish. It seems to me that people in the past who made a great fuss in denouncing the superstitious ways of another people in comparison with their own simply wasted their time and energy. After all, there is no fundamental difference between one people and another. Yet the stressing of differences between peoples is still pursued, and it is always so between individuals. That is one large mystery of life which still remains.

I cannot help thinking how courtship has changed in China just as we have discarded our four-poster beds for divans. Under the domination of Confucius' teaching of the moral law, boys and girls were not supposed to be seen together. Nevertheless, there were many ways of courting and throwing-a-handkerchief-with-a-verse-on-it was one of the common practices. The picking-up-handkerchief tactics have long been replaced by joining hands, or whispering under a tree or in some darkish corner. Recently a young Chinese doctor friend of mine told me that he had only had one and a half dates with his girl, for on the first date she had her parents with her so that it could only be counted as a half. This amazed and amused me, but I could see our human life becoming plainer than ever. In essence life has always been very plain and I am sure that there must have been many of our young men who could have said the same thing as the one in the following hundred-year-old Chinese joke:

A young man who had seen his girl almost every day had been called away to a distant place. When they met again each swore to the other that they had been thinking of one another all the time. "Not a night," claimed the girl, "that I did not dream of being with you and going about with you. This was caused by my constant thoughts of you." She repeated and repeated this until the youth felt a little uncomfortable, for she did not inquire after his health in the distant land at all. "Well, my dear," remarked the youth, "I too have been dreaming of you." The girl became excited and kept asking what kind of dreams he had had. "To tell you the truth, what I dreamt was that you were not dreaming of me."

To rouse Hsien-Ch'i I told him what I learned about a romantic story of Marblehead. It happened that in the Colonial days a handsome English officer, Sir Harry Frankland, was the resident Collector of the Port of Boston for the King's government. He came to Marblehead on a personal matter but caught sight of a pretty young girl scrubbing dirty door-steps from the window of the house where he was staying. She was the orphan daughter of a Marblehead sailor lost at sea, and was named Agnes Surriage. Her beauty stirred the handsome officer's heart and he thought she should not spend her time scrubbing. He soon bought all the necessary fashionable clothes to dress the girl up and to send her to study in Boston. Being only fifteen, the young thing felt grateful, and delighted. After her schooling she met her benefactor again, and her beauty in young womanhood dazzled him even more. He fell in love with her, while she out of gratitude accepted the love as a matter of course. Unfortunately the noble blood in Sir Harry barred him from taking a sailor's daughter as a wife. Nevertheless he built a mansion to house her in Hopkinton until they were driven away to Portugal by the local poisonous tongues. In Portugal in 1755 Sir Harry was badly hurt under a fallen wall during the great earthquake, and he was dug out by the tender hands of the girl. Then they were legally married. To have saved his life elevated the scrubbing girl into Lady Frankland. Hsien-Ch'i laughed at the stupidity of not marrying her for love but for her heroic deed. But I remarked that time and circumstance should be taken into consideration in judging the matter. They might not have to move away from Hopkinton had they lived today.

By now those who had been fishing had gone. A few people were still sitting on the iron bars and on the rocks. None made any movement. There was a complete stillness in the air, yet the broad bosom of the sea kept up its equal motion, swelling and sinking in large curves. The only sound we heard was the lapping of the water against the rocks. The tide was coming in and foam flakes flew around. The white sails were fewer but more distinct against the deep blue sea. They looked anchored, yet changed positions as if someone was playing draughts on the sea-board. Or they seemed to assume the shape of oversized seagulls. The far horizon that had been clear to my eyes a moment ago could be discerned no more. Darkness began to reign. It was time to go back to Boston. But the lingering faint twilight over the horizon indicated more mysteries of life yet to be discovered. I suggested that we look for the Colonel Jeremiah Lee Mansion, that was built before the American Revolution, as it is regarded as the pride of Marblehead, but it eluded us. My friend drove slowly through the narrow, twisting streets and lanes. The town folk had long gone indoors for their evening meal and all was quiet.

Provincetown

The sky is high, the sea wide, no boundary in sight;
For more than three hundred years these shores must
    have been lapped or lashed and foaming.
Temporarily the Pilgrims set their bodies down to rest;
How could they know that from that moment
    they would build a nation
And make all everywhere friendly and happy?
Is it not praise-worthy?

What has been going on in my Eastern land?
Year after year turmoil and entanglement?
Standing on the sand
I ask the floating sunset.

樸落芽斯鎮

天空海濶少涯
三百年來此岸拍花當
時權把身多下些知
從此後組國家民和
集此怎不堪誇何多
我東土歲亂麻多
麻主平沙且汹流霞

XIX

Boston Spirit

S E E I N G Boston without seeing Plymouth, thirty-seven
miles southeast of Boston, did not satisfy me, so I went
there twice, first with my artist friend, Tseng Hsien-Ch'i, and
again by myself. It was during my second visit to Plymouth
that I got a clear notion of what I mean by the spirit of
Boston.

The first visit took place on a warm Friday morning in
August when our car stopped at the common parking ground.
The sun was hidden somewhere inside the clouds, but everything looked bright and fresh in the clear sea air. We followed a number of visitors into the neatly thatched hut, a
replica of the Settler's home, right close to the sea-shore. We
bought a few cards from a smooth-skinned young girl in a
freshly-laundered Pilgrim costume. We were then entertained with an account of the landing on Plymouth Rock
in 1620 by a boy of eighteen clad in a Pilgrim-cut shirt
and trousers of coloured silk and a Pilgrim hat. Another
young boy in the uniform of Pilgrim days with a long
spear dashed down the wooden stairs, while we went up
to the open roof of a replica of an old Plymouth Fort,
part of which was still in construction. We had a look at
Plymouth Harbor and the Church of the Pilgrimage from
Cole's Hill. Hsien-Ch'i took a photograph of the statue of
Massasoit and of the Memorial Fountain "in Memory of the
Heroic Women of the Mayflower 1620–1920." The statue of
the "Pilgrim Maid" and the pool in the Brewster Gardens

detained us longer. We walked up the wooden steps to see the old Leyden Street houses and peeped inside Pilgrim Hall Museum after having found Howland House, the only house left in Plymouth where Pilgrims once lived. On our way down from the National Monument to the Forefathers,

Plymouth Rock

we encountered a stream of people in the costumes of three hundred years ago, though newly-tailored. We were told that it was the "Pilgrims' Progress" presented by the Plymouth Antiquarian Society every summer.

Two months later I reached Plymouth by rail and walked to the peristyle over Plymouth Rock. Only one visitor came after me, who read aloud the date, 1620, on the rock and left again in a moment. There was no sign of the boy in the Pilgrim costume, nor anything inside the peristyle. The Rock was clear and serene. I sat down between two pillars with my back against one of them and gazed at the vast expanse of the sea—so much activity, yet so peaceful. My mind was full, for I had now read something about Plymouth. I began to ponder why and how the Pilgrims came to set their feet on the Rock.

The English Pilgrims came to North America with an idea, a principle, and almost their bare hands. They did hire Myles Standish as their protector. He was neither a Puritan nor a genuine Pilgrim, but he proved to be a brave man of outstanding character. The old record says of Captain Standish and many others in the Pilgrim group:

> . . . to their great commendation be it spoken, spared no pains night nor day, but with abundance of toyle and hazard of their own strength helped others in sickness and death, a rare example worthy to be remembered.

This tells me that the group of one-hundred-and-four Mayflower passengers was a community of good people. Only in such a community could the goodness of one like Captain Standish be recognized with certainty. I am not always inclined to be skeptical, but in our modern community of men with all the ingenious methods of write-up can we really know who is good and who is not? Not that a good man wishes to be recognized, nor that there is no man like Captain Standish in our community, whether it be American, English, or Chinese, but that we now seem, broadly speaking, to be incapable of standing up for what we feel is good. I only wish the Pilgrims' spirit still reigned among us.

Yet I doubt whether in everyday matters the human nature of the Pilgrims can really have been so different from ours and I am quite sure that there must have been dissensions among some of them during their miserable, tempestuous voyage of sixty-six days within the crowded space of a ship ninety feet long and with a beam of twenty-six feet.

When food became less interesting and less hygienic, sickness and death occurred; resentment and grumbling must have arisen on the way and after landing at Plymouth. But these people had *a principle,* a common faith in which they strongly believed. They wanted to find a place where they could live within the freedom of the faith they held. It was this faith which bound them together with tolerance and gave them an undaunted spirit in the face of unimaginable hardships. I do not remember hearing or reading of any similar occurrence in China's history. We have single and scattered cases of some noted scholar-statesman dying for Confucius' principle of loyalty to sovereignty. To sacrifice one's life for a principle is not equal to risking one's life for the continuation of a faith. I may be wrong in thinking that few of the one-hundred-and-four Mayflower passengers were noted personalities of the time, but from what I have read, it seems that they were mostly ordinary, simple folk, who risked their lives for their belief. This is unheard-of in Chinese history. Someone may have read the translation of a famous Chinese novel *Shui Hu Chuan* or "All Men are Brothers," as Pearl Buck translates it, and may think that those one hundred and eight men in the novel who combatted the wrongdoers were comparable. But they were fictional figures, and their work more like that of Robin Hood than in the Pilgrim spirit.

China's history is full of tyrannical oppression exercised over the Chinese people at one time or another. One of the most tyrannical oppressions that was ever staged in China was the Literary Inquisition of Emperor Ch'ien-lung (1736–1795). Even the slightest hint of a criticism of the Manchu ruler caused the writer's head to be cut off, his family and even his relations and friends to suffer a similar fate together, while the books he had written and collected would be burned.

It was a great pity that the Pilgrims' spirit was not known in the Far East, otherwise a number of Chinese people might have fled the tyrannical oppression of the Literary Inquisition, and built a new China somewhere in the Pacific like New England in the Atlantic. But would they? In the first place we Chinese are not a seafaring people. Most Chinese peasants and working folk can endure and have endured any hardship but they have never been fired by a great faith, for which to stand firm. Besides, to my way of thinking, few learned men in the whole history of China have shown courage and tolerance; though some died for a principle, yet not for a faith like the leaders of the Pilgrims. However, the innate love of freedom in the Chinese is as great as in any other race. Chinese history has shown the downfall of tyrannical rulers every one or more hundred years. Much suffering was endured and much blood shed at each change of dynasty. I wish we Chinese could now study the Pilgrims' spirit and be inspired to combine all our efforts for the common good of man instead of just trying to pull down one dynasty after another. Here I pay my homage to all the Pilgrims who set their feet on the Plymouth Rock.

It is known that the *Speedwell,* though she sailed with the *Mayflower* from Southhampton, never left English shores, but that the *Mayflower* carried the one hundred and four passengers through a tempestuous voyage of sixty-six days to their first proper washday at Provincetown on Monday, November 21, 1620. The following spring half of them were dead. The rest struggled hard for mere existence from almost barren land to a good harvest. Thus began the Thanksgiving Day Festival of America. Thanksgiving Day is exclusively

American. It has been observed by the Americans for the past three hundred years.

To be sure of enough to eat for the days to come after a whole year of toil on an empty stomach must have made the first Pilgrims wild and even hysterical with joy. But their strong faith and their undaunted spirit kept them in check. Before the first Thanksgiving Day the scrupulous distribution of the scanty amount of food for daily use must have put a tremendous strain on the very few who were in charge. I may be wrong to presume that these very few would be the twenty or so women in the whole party of one hundred and four. Several of the twenty were mere young girls, and several others contracted disease and died before or soon after their arrival at Plymouth. The rest of the women played their part with thrift, sternness, and fairness, while their men toiled with courage and single-mindedness first in keeping the *Mayflower* floating and then in growing food on the land of their first settlement. I am not in a position to discuss nor describe the hardships that the Pilgrims endured, but I know that their story would be different if there had been no women in their midst to manage the daily trifles and to check their tempers at times with sternness and fairness.

A well-brought-up and fair-minded woman is always the backbone of the sound traditions of a good society, for it is she who will have the stern courage to keep good order, disregarding its consequences to herself. I may be a little biassed in saying this, for I saw this stern courage in my own grandmother, who managed a big family of forty members living under one roof, as I described in my book *A Chinese Childhood*. Throughout the whole history of China many a good woman contributed much to the success of wise rulers, but left no famous name behind; yet many of those who ruined one dynasty after another are still known by name to us to the present day. Thinking of all this I could not help paying my own tribute to the "Heroic Women of the Mayflower."

I think the female side of the American spiritual ancestors still blooms in the women of Boston. I have met a few Boston ladies of nearly ninety years of age or more. They still sit as upright as if they were in a Victorian high-backed chair and still talk in a stern voice and with a thrifty outlook in economic dealings. I admit that I laughed when I was told that a Boston lady would insist on going round the world by way of Dedham, but her dauntless courage in pursuing her aim has my admiration. We must not forget what the early women Pilgrims as well as the early Boston women have done for the stability of American society.

The following words written to his father by John Quincy Adams at the age of nine illustrate my point:

Dear Sir:

I love to receive letters very well; much better than I love to write them. I make but a poor figure at composition. My head is much too fickle. My thoughts are running after bird's eggs, play and trifles, till I get vexed with myself. Mamma has a troublesome task to keep me astudying . . .

Though the second President of the United States wanted to bring his son up in a great tradition, it was the young boy's mama who had the troublesome task of keeping him studying so that he became a great statesman and the sixth president of the country. Mrs. John Adams contributed no less than her husband to the shaping of America. The part played by the great Boston families from the early Colonial days to the present has been invaluable. I come from a country where the centuries-old tradition has always been revered, and I appreciate this Boston heritage all the more as I see the old Chinese tradition disintegrating.

To write such a letter as the above at the tender age of nine is admirable. John Quincy Adams' mother must have been keeping her son at his studies almost as soon as he could talk. We have stories of many a clever boy able to recite and even compose good poetry at a very young age in the history of China, but it has not been easy to hear of such clever ones within the past hundred years or so, for China has had so many troubles. Strangely enough, I was interviewed by a young Boston boy of eight for nearly an hour when I stayed with the Van Wyck Brooks at Bridgewater, Connecticut. Mrs. Brooks' grandson, Tommy Saltonstall, was spending his Easter vacation there. He said that his school was having a lesson about China and he wanted to ask me a number of questions, so that he could give some information to his class when he returned to school. For a moment I did not know what to say, for I have always dreaded meeting an interviewer, as I feel that I have no reason to be interviewed, a point of view which my publishers in England and America often refuse to understand. There was no way out this time. Tommy started drafting his questionnaire and then typed it on a few sheets of paper. By the look of the bundle in his hand I knew that the interview was going to be a lengthy one. I had to answer many points about China's climate, size, population, mountains, rivers and lakes, the clothes worn and the food eaten, etc. Finally Tommy asked me: "Which is your fondest memory of China?" "My grandmother!" was my quick answer. He smiled and stood up to shake hands with me. And we became good friends from that day.

After having delivered a lecture on "How a Chinese artist paints" at Cornell University in October, 1956, I met Professor Clinton Rossiter through our mutual friend, Professor Harold Shadick of the same university, when we boarded the same plane for New York. I soon learned that Professor Rossiter's ancestors came to settle in New England from Old England in 1630 and that his family name was later changed from Rochester into Rossiter. We found out that we have a number of mutual friends in Boston. It is in one of Professor

My young interviewer

Rossiter's books, *The First American Revolution,* that I find my ideas of the Boston spirit reinforced:

The wilderness demanded of those who would conquer it that they spend their lives in unremitting toil. Unable to devote any sizable part of their energies to government, the settlers insisted that government let them alone and perform its severely limited tasks at the amateur level. The early American definition of liberty as freedom *from* government was given added popularity and meaning by frontier conditions. It was a new and invigorating experience for tens of thousands of Englishmen, Germans, and Scotch-Irish to be able to build a home where they would at last be "let alone."

This "let alone" liberty was the cherished hope of the great sixth-century B.C. Chinese philosopher, Lao Tzu, whose principle was *Wu-wei* meaning "non-action" or "Non-interference"; the government should not do anything that might jeopardise the people's peaceful pursuit of life. Such a non-action government has never come into being in China and the Chinese people have therefore always been under tyrannical oppression in one manner or another. Why has America succeeded in having a government "of the people, by the people and for the people"? Professor Rossiter also enlightened me on this point:

The wilderness did not itself create democracy; indeed, it often encouraged the growth of ideas and institutions hostile to it. But it did help to produce some of the raw materials of American democracy—self-reliance, social fluidity, simplicity, equality, dislike of privilege, optimism, and devotion to liberty. At the same time, it emphasized the importance of voluntary co-operation. The group, too, had its uses on the frontier, whether for defence or barn-raising or cornhusking. The phrases "free association," "mutual subjection," and "the wilderness" . . .

All these raw materials had their roots in Boston. It was the first Bostonians who gave the early American definition of liberty as freedom *from* government. If I understand it correctly, "freedom from government" does not mean no government, but a government functioning without unnecessary and unreasonable interference with the people.

During my few months' stay in Boston in 1953 there was a very uneasy air created by the measures against un-American activities not only in Boston but everywhere in the

United States. It had nothing to do with my travels, but
the topic often came into conversations. There was tension.
When I went back to Oxford, England, I was frequently
asked about the matter, as if a new type of tyranny had
arisen in America. Later I came to New York again in the
fall of 1955 and paid visits to Boston from time to time. That

Joseph Welch, 1955–1956 fighter for freedom

uneasy air that had existed more than a year before had been
dispersed. Mr. Joseph Welch, a famous Boston lawyer, was
making a strong stand for liberty of human rights and was
ensuring that "freedom from government" would be maintained. Long before that, the new President of Harvard
University, Dr. Nathan M. Pusey, took the lead in his quiet
manner to ward off governmental interference from the
three-centuries-old freedom of American learning. The Boston spirit of love of universal liberty had acted again. The
Boston spirit is very much alive still. In viewing a third type
of "ideological" tyranny that has confronted most modern
men I value my own find of the Boston spirit and I hope it
will inspire many to make their stand for the love of universal liberty.